VISTAS

An Interactive Course in English

1

Project Director   H. Douglas Brown

Senior Writers
Tony Silva
Sharon Seymour
Pamela Polos

Contributing Writers
Amelia Kreitzer
Bradley Reed
Nancy Schaefer
Jean Svacina
Kathy Varchetto

REGENTS/PRENTICE HALL
Englewood Cliffs, New Jersey 07632

Library of Congress Cataloging-in-Publication Data

Brown, H. Douglas, 1941–
    Vistas: an interactive course in English / H. Douglas Brown.
    p.   cm.

    ISBN 0-13-650326-8 (student book: v. 1)
    1. English language—Textbooks for foreign speakers.   I.
    Title.
PE1128.B725 1991
428.2′4—dc20
                                  90-44440
                                      CIP

Publisher: Tina B. Carver
Development Manager: Mary Vaughn
Senior Editor: Larry Anger
Development Editor: Louisa B. Hellegers
Audio Editor: Stephanie Karras
Production and Editorial Supervisor: Janet S. Johnston
Design Director: Janet Schmid
Pre-Press Buyer: Ray Keating
Manufacturing Buyer: Lori Bulwin
Scheduler: Leslie Coward
Interior and Cover Designer: Suzanne Bennett

Illustrators: Glenn Davis, Don Martinetti
Cover Photo: Wm. Ervin/Comstock
Audio Production: Phyllis Dolgin

ISBN 0-13-650326-8

Prentice-Hall International (UK) Limited, *London*
Prentice-Hall of Australia Pty. Limited, *Sydney*
Prentice-Hall Canada Inc., *Toronto*
Prentice-Hall Hispanoamericana, S.A., *Mexico*
Prentice-Hall of India Private Limited, *New Delhi*
Prentice-Hall of Japan, Inc., *Tokyo*
Simon & Schuster Asia Pte. Ltd., *Singapore*
Editora Prentice-Hall do Brasil, Ltda., *Rio de Janeiro*

Photo Credits

All photos by Laima Druskis except:
  page 46: Frenchwoman—*Vincent Hazat/Photo Researchers*
       47: Bill Cosby and Eddie Murphy—*Lynn Goldsmith/LGI*
           Michael Chang—*Michael Baz/ProServ*
           Kenny Rogers—*Kelly Junkermann/*
           Rogers & Cowan, Inc.
           Michelle Pfeiffer—*PMK Inc.*
           Arnold Schwarzenegger and Danny DeVito—
             Universal/Shooting Star
           Diana, Princess of Wales—*British Information Service*
           Barbara Bush—*Carol T. Powers/The White House*
           Gloria Estefan—*Brian Smith/Shooting Star*
       58: Boston in winter—*Eunice Harris/Photo Researchers*
           Boston in spring, summer, and fall—
             Massachusetts Division of Tourism
       95: two men/monkey—*Photofest*
           horror movie still—*Photofest*
     124: coins—*Page Poore*

Field Testers and Reviewers

Prentice Hall Regents would like to thank the following field
testers and reviewers of *Vistas*, whose insights and suggestions
helped to shape the content and format of the series: Julia
Berenguer de Soltice, Valencia, Spain; Walther Bolzmann,
Coordinator of Evaluation, *TRANSLEX*, Lima, Peru; Mary Ann
Corley, ESOL Outreach Advisor, Adult Basic Education,
Baltimore County Public School, Towson, Maryland; Barbara
Goodwin, *SCS Institute*, New York, New York; Madeline
Hudders, *University of Puerto Rico*, San Juan, Puerto Rico;
Gloria Kismadi, Director of Courses, *Limbaga Amerika*,
Jakarta, Indonesia; Walter Lockhart, *Lockhart Group*,
Pamplona, Spain; Lydia Lopez, *University of Puerto Rico*, San
Juan, Puerto Rico; Janet Nieves, *Instituto Cultural
Domenico-Americano*, Santo Domingo, Dominican Republic;
Jaime Ponce, Executive Director, *TRANSLEX*, Lima, Peru;
Martin Roman, Director, *Instituto Cultural Dominico-Americano*,
Santo Domingo, Dominican Republic; Helen Slivka, New York,
New York; Daniel Soltice, Valencia, Spain; Carmen Zapata,
University of Puerto Rico, San Juan, Puerto Rico.

CONTENTS

Topics and Skills

Meeting people
Completing an I.D. card

Grammar

Subject pronouns (**I, he, she, it, we, you, they**)
Present tense of **be**
    information (wh-) questions with **where** and
    what
    affirmative statements
    contractions (**'m, 's, 're**)
Prepositions (**from, in**)

Communication Goals

Greeting people
Introducing yourself
Exchanging personal information
Saying goodbye
Asking how to spell something
Thanking

Topics and Skills

The classroom
Telephone numbers and addresses
Completing a registration form
Making an address book

Grammar

Demonstratives (**this, that, these, those**)
Indefinite article (**a, an**)
Singular vs. plural nouns (**pen, pens**)
Present tense of **be**
    information (wh-) questions
    affirmative and negative statements
    yes/no questions and short answers

Communication Goals

Identifying and asking for names of objects
Correcting and confirming
Exchanging personal information
Asking about class
Thanking
Apologizing

Topics and Skills

The family
Occupations
Physical characteristics
Writing a personal description

Grammar

Possessive adjectives (**my, his, her, its, our, your, their**)
Possessive **'s**
Present tense of **be**
    information (wh-) questions
    negative statements
Affirmative statements with **have**
Adjectives (**pretty, blue,** etc.)

Communication Goals

Identifying and describing people
Exchanging personal information
Exchanging information about other people
Getting someone's attention
Asking someone to repeat something
Talking about possessions

Topics and Skills

The home and furniture
Seasons and weather
Dates
Writing a postcard

Grammar

Prepositions (**in, on, under, over, next to, behind, in front of, between, around**)
There is and **There are**
    affirmative and negative statements
    yes/no questions
Present tense of **be**
    information (wh-) questions
    questions with **or**
Some and **any** with count nouns
Definite article (**the**)

Communication Goals

Describing things and their locations
Describing differences
Talking about quantity
Asking for and giving locations
Talking about the weather and the seasons
Asking for and giving dates

Topics and Skills

Present activities
Clothes and colors
Reading abbreviations
Reading *For Rent* ads
Reading a map

Grammar

Present continuous tense
    affirmative and negative statements
    yes/no questions
    information (wh-) questions
Prepositions (**at, to, on the corner of, across from**)
Regular and irregular plurals (**dresses, libraries, scarves, women**)

Communication Goals

Talking about the present
Talking about clothes and colors
Talking on the telephone
Asking for and giving locations

Topics and Skills

Days of the week and daily routines
Writing a letter about someone's family, work, and interests

Grammar

Simple present tense
    affirmative and negative statements
    yes/no questions
    short answers
Prepositions (**on, near**)
Conjunction (**but**)

Communication Goals

Asking for and giving the day
Telling about your week
Finding out about people's schedules
Asking about relatives and friends
Explaining differences

UNIT 7 86

Topics and Skills

The time
Work and transportation
Movies
Reading a bus schedule
Understanding recorded movie announcements

Grammar

Simple present tense: information (wh-) questions
Too and **either**
Adverbs of manner (slow**ly**, careful**ly**, **well,
fast,** etc.)
Clauses with **before, after,** and **when**

Communication Goals

Asking and telling the time
Offering help
Asking for transportation information
Talking about work or school
Describing how people do things
Contrasting
Talking about movies
Agreeing

UNIT 8 98

Topics and Skills

Work and chores
Leisure time
Reading entertainment ads
Writing a note to a friend

Grammar

Adverbs of frequency (**usually, sometimes,
always,** etc.)
The simple present vs. the present continuous tense
Have to
   affirmative and negative statements
   yes/no questions
   information (wh-) questions
Conjunction **(because)**
Let's

Communication Goals

Talking about how often people do things
Comparing
Talking about what people have to do
Asking why and giving reasons and opinions
Making suggestions and accepting or declining

UNIT 9 110

Topics and Skills

Cooking, shopping, and food
Reading food ads
Making a shopping list
Reading recipes

Grammar

Count and non-count nouns (**tomato, tomatoes,
rice,** etc.)
Some and **any**
A lot of, much, and **many**
Questions with **how much** and **how many**
Quantities (**a box of, a dozen,** etc.)
Imperative (**Put . . .**)

Communication Goals

Talking about availability
Talking about quantities
Asking for locations in a grocery store
Asking about prices
Talking about favorite things

UNIT 10 122

Topics and Skills

Vending machines and money
Restaurants
The future
Reading a menu
Reading a restaurant check

Grammar

Affirmative and negative imperative (**Push . . ./ Don't push . . .**)
Verb + **to** + verb (**want to go, need to buy,** etc.)
The future with the present progressive
Expressions of future time (**later, tomorrow, next week,** etc.)

Communication Goals

Asking for change
Giving and following instructions
Making suggestions
Talking about the future
Giving opinions
Ordering in a restaurant

GETTING STARTED

1 Hello and goodbye 📼

Hello		Goodbye
Hi.	Good morning.	Goodbye. (Bye.)
Hello.	Good afternoon.	Good night.
	Good evening.	See you tomorrow.

1

2 The students, the teacher, and the alphabet ▭

Aa	Bb	Cc	Dd	Ee	Ff	Gg	Hh	Ii
Jj	Kk	Ll	Mm	Nn	Oo	Pp	Qq	Rr
Ss	Tt	Uu	Vv	Ww	Xx	Yy	Zz	

1 Roberto	8 Yon Mi
2 Pierre	9 Keiko
3 Tetsuo	10 Oscar
4 Gina	11 Marco
5 Pravit	12 Tony
6 Lucy	13 Olga
7 Carlos	14 Lynn

A: **What's your name?**
B: **My name is** *Pierre.*

A: **Spell your name.**
B: *P-i-e-r-r-e.*

3 The classroom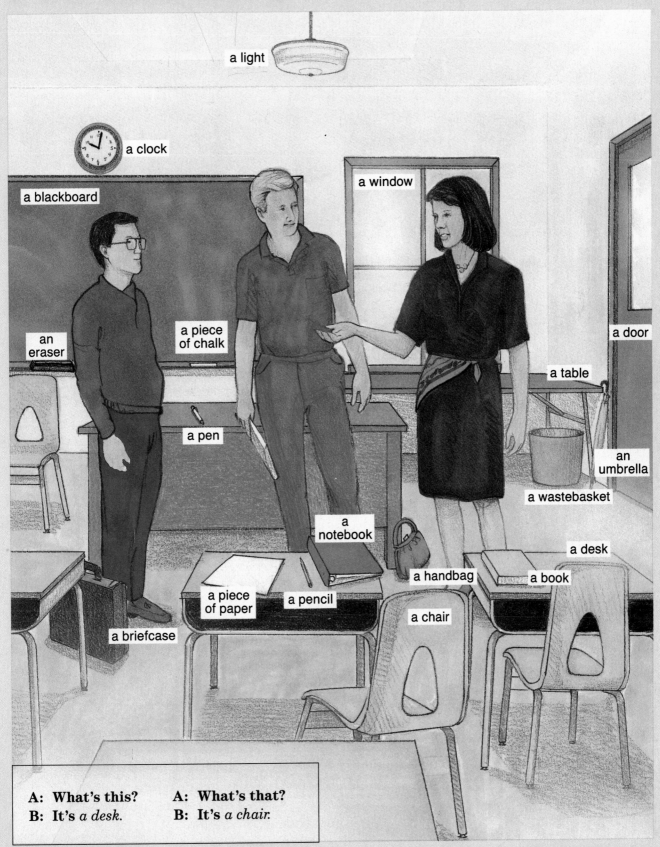

a light

a clock

a window

a blackboard

a piece of chalk

an eraser

a door

a table

a pen

an umbrella

a wastebasket

a notebook

a desk

a handbag

a book

a piece of paper

a pencil

a chair

a briefcase

A: **What's this?**
B: It's *a desk.*

A: **What's that?**
B: It's *a chair.*

4 Useful phrases

Say your name.	Read number *1*.	Close your book.
Listen.	Go to the blackboard.	Ask your partner.
Open your book to page *4*.	Write the question.	I don't understand.
Look at the picture.	Answer the question.	

5 Occupations

a waitress

an actor

a reporter

a police officer

a secretary

an actress

a mechanic

an architect

a waiter

a photographer

a computer programmer

a doctor

a security guard

a nurse

a carpenter

a teacher

A: **What's her occupation?**
B: **She's** *a photographer.*

A: **What's his occupation?**
B: **He's** *an architect.*

A: **What's your occupation?**
B: **I'm** *a student.*

6 Cardinal numbers 📼

0 zero	10 ten	20 twenty	30 thirty
1 one	11 eleven	21 twenty-one	40 forty
2 two	12 twelve	22 twenty-two	50 fifty
3 three	13 thirteen	23 twenty-three	60 sixty
4 four	14 fourteen	24 twenty-four	70 seventy
5 five	15 fifteen	25 twenty-five	80 eighty
6 six	16 sixteen	26 twenty-six	90 ninety
7 seven	17 seventeen	27 twenty-seven	100 one hundred
8 eight	18 eighteen	28 twenty-eight	1,000 one thousand
9 nine	19 nineteen	29 twenty-nine	

A: **Count from** *1* **to** *10.*
B: *1, 2, 3, 4, 5, 6, 7, 8, 9, 10.*

A: **How much is** *10* **plus** *10*?
B: *10 plus 10 is 20.*

7 The United States and Canada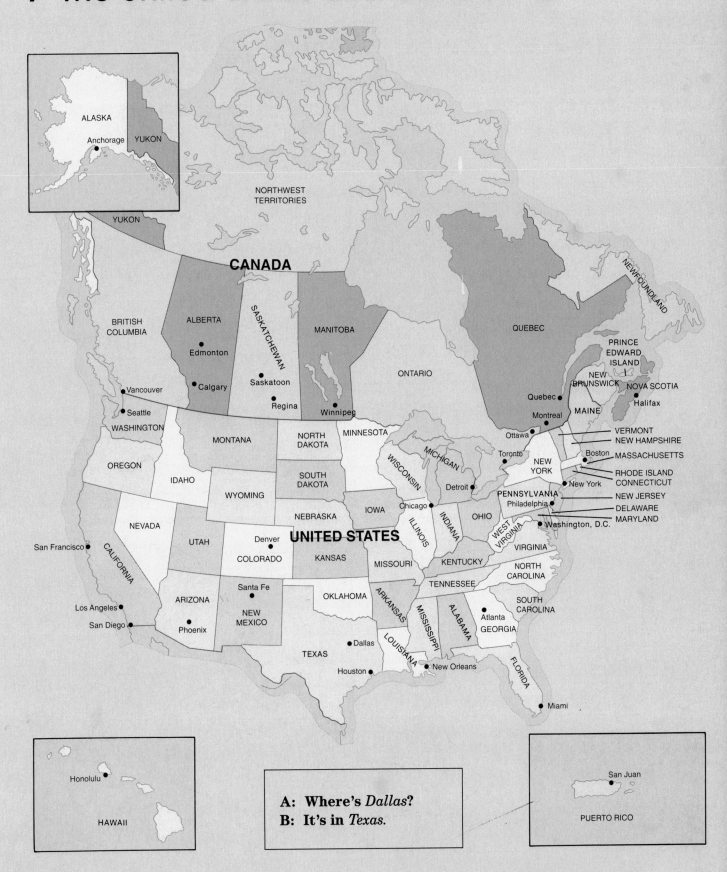

ALASKA

Anchorage

YUKON

YUKON

NORTHWEST
TERRITORIES

CANADA

BRITISH
COLUMBIA

ALBERTA

Edmonton

• Calgary

SASKATCHEWAN

Saskatoon •

Regina •

MANITOBA

Winnipeg •

ONTARIO

QUEBEC

NEWFOUNDLAND

PRINCE
EDWARD
ISLAND

NEW
BRUNSWICK

NOVA SCOTIA

Halifax •

Quebec •

Montreal •

MAINE

Vancouver •

• Seattle

WASHINGTON

MONTANA

NORTH
DAKOTA

MINNESOTA

MICHIGAN

WISCONSIN

Toronto •

Ottawa •

VERMONT

NEW HAMPSHIRE

Boston •

MASSACHUSETTS

OREGON

IDAHO

SOUTH
DAKOTA

WYOMING

NEBRASKA

IOWA

Chicago •

ILLINOIS

INDIANA

OHIO

Detroit •

NEW
YORK

PENNSYLVANIA

Philadelphia •

RHODE ISLAND

CONNECTICUT

New York •

NEW JERSEY

DELAWARE

MARYLAND

• Washington, D.C.

San Francisco •

NEVADA

UTAH

Denver •

COLORADO

KANSAS

MISSOURI

KENTUCKY

UNITED STATES

WEST
VIRGINIA

VIRGINIA

CALIFORNIA

ARIZONA

Santa Fe •

NEW
MEXICO

OKLAHOMA

ARKANSAS

TENNESSEE

NORTH
CAROLINA

SOUTH
CAROLINA

Los Angeles •

San Diego •

Phoenix •

TEXAS

• Dallas

Houston •

MISSISSIPPI

LOUISIANA

New Orleans •

ALABAMA

Atlanta •

GEORGIA

FLORIDA

Miami •

Honolulu •

HAWAII

A: **Where's** *Dallas*?
B: **It's in** *Texas*.

San Juan •

PUERTO RICO

8 The world ▭

I'm from Canada.

I'm from the United States.

I'm from Mexico.

I'm from Puerto Rico.

I'm from Colombia.

I'm from Chile.

I'm from Brazil.

I'm from Spain.

I'm from Italy.

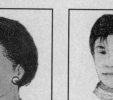

I'm from Nigeria.

I'm from China.

I'm from Japan.

I'm from Thailand.

GREENLAND

CANADA

HAWAII

UNITED STATES OF AMERICA

MEXICO

BAHAMAS

CUBA
HAITI
DOMINICAN REPUBLIC
PUERTO RICO

GUATEMALA — BELIZE
JAMAICA
DOMINICA
BARBADOS
EL SALVADOR — HONDURAS
NICARAGUA
TRINIDAD AND TOBAGO
COSTA RICA
VENEZUELA GUYANA
PANAMA
SURINAM
COLOMBIA
FRENCH GUIANA

ECUADOR

PERU

BRAZIL

BOLIVIA

PARAGUAY

CHILE

ARGENTINA

URUGUAY

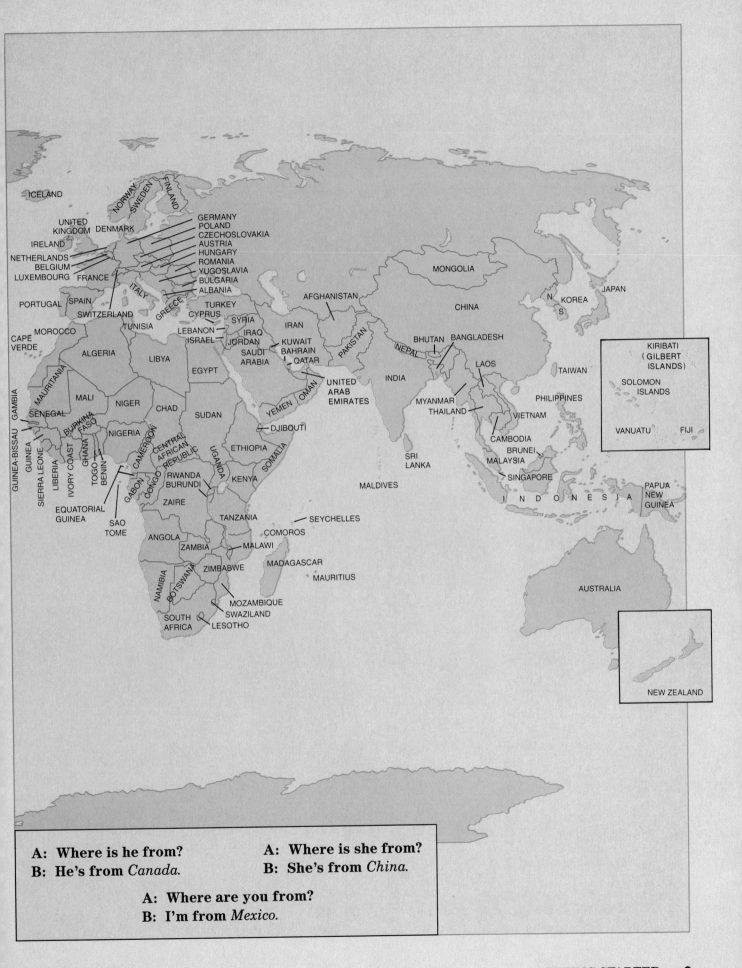

ICELAND

NORWAY SWEDEN FINLAND

UNITED KINGDOM DENMARK GERMANY POLAND CZECHOSLOVAKIA AUSTRIA HUNGARY ROMANIA YUGOSLAVIA BULGARIA ALBANIA

IRELAND

NETHERLANDS BELGIUM LUXEMBOURG FRANCE

PORTUGAL SPAIN ITALY GREECE TURKEY CYPRUS SYRIA

SWITZERLAND TUNISIA LEBANON ISRAEL JORDAN IRAN

MOROCCO CAPE VERDE ALGERIA LIBYA EGYPT SAUDI ARABIA KUWAIT BAHRAIN QATAR

MONGOLIA

AFGHANISTAN CHINA N KOREA S JAPAN

PAKISTAN NEPAL BHUTAN BANGLADESH

TAIWAN

INDIA LAOS

UNITED ARAB EMIRATES MYANMAR THAILAND PHILIPPINES

YEMEN OMAN VIETNAM

GAMBIA GUINEA-BISSAU GUINEA SIERRA LEONE LIBERIA IVORY COAST

MAURITANIA MALI NIGER CHAD SUDAN DJIBOUTI

SENEGAL BURKINA FASO NIGERIA CENTRAL AFRICAN REPUBLIC ETHIOPIA SOMALIA SRI LANKA CAMBODIA BRUNEI MALAYSIA SINGAPORE

GHANA TOGO BENIN CAMEROON GABON CONGO UGANDA KENYA RWANDA BURUNDI MALDIVES INDONESIA

EQUATORIAL GUINEA SAO TOME ZAIRE TANZANIA SEYCHELLES PAPUA NEW GUINEA

ANGOLA ZAMBIA MALAWI COMOROS

NAMIBIA ZIMBABWE MADAGASCAR MAURITIUS AUSTRALIA

BOTSWANA MOZAMBIQUE SWAZILAND

SOUTH AFRICA LESOTHO

KIRIBATI (GILBERT ISLANDS)

SOLOMON ISLANDS

VANUATU FIJI

NEW ZEALAND

A: **Where is he from?**
B: **He's from** *Canada.*

A: **Where is she from?**
B: **She's from** *China.*

A: **Where are you from?**
B: **I'm from** *Mexico.*

9 Colors and clothes ▭

BLUE YELLOW **PURPLE** PINK BROWN **BLACK**
RED GREEN ORANGE GRAY BEIGE WHITE

a shirt

a skirt

gloves

a coat

a hat

a scarf

glasses

a jacket

a tie

pants

a dress

a belt

a sweater

sunglasses

a suit

a blouse

a T-shirt

shorts

socks

shoes

A: **What color is** *the suit*?
B: **It's** *blue*.

A: **What color are** *the shorts*?
B: **They're** *yellow*.

10 The house

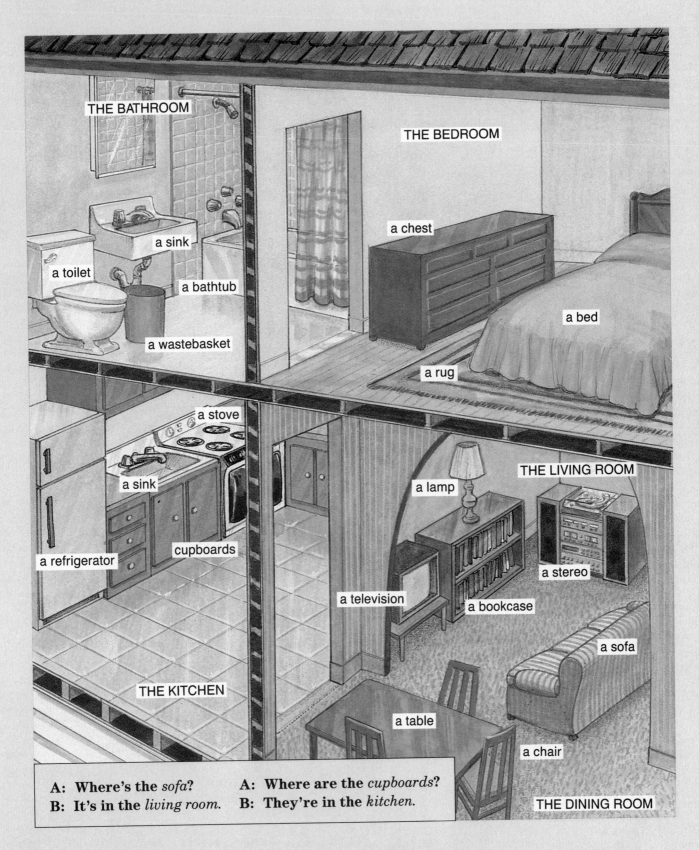

THE BATHROOM
a sink
a toilet
a bathtub
a wastebasket

THE BEDROOM
a chest
a bed
a rug

a stove
a sink
cupboards
a refrigerator
THE KITCHEN

a lamp
THE LIVING ROOM
a stereo
a television
a bookcase
a sofa
a table
a chair
THE DINING ROOM

A: **Where's the** *sofa*?
B: **It's in the** *living room*.

A: **Where are the** *cupboards*?
B: **They're in the** *kitchen*.

11 Ann Brennan's family

grandfather

grandmother

father

mother

husband

Ann (wife)

sister

brother

son

daughter

Look at this picture.	Show a picture of your family.
A: Who's that? B: That's Ann's *mother*.	A: Who's that? B: That's my *mother*.

12 Physical characteristics 📼

Mary Arden
short

Alice Arden
average height

Judy Arden
tall

Henry Arden
fat

Michael Arden
average weight

Jim Arden
thin

blond hair
blue eyes

brown hair
green eyes
a mustache

black hair
brown eyes

red hair
gray eyes
a beard

gray hair
blue eyes

A: **Describe** *Judy Arden*.
B: **She's** *tall.* **She has** *blond* **hair and** *blue* **eyes.**

A: **Describe** *Michael Arden*.
B: **He's** *average weight.* **He has** *red* **hair,** *gray* **eyes, and** *a beard.*

A: **Describe yourself.**
B: **I'm** *short,* **and I have** *brown* **hair and** *brown* **eyes.**

13 Food 🔲

VEGETABLES
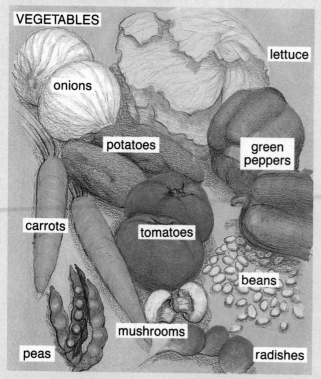
- onions
- lettuce
- potatoes
- green peppers
- carrots
- tomatoes
- beans
- peas
- mushrooms
- radishes

FRUIT

- oranges
- apples
- bananas
- pears
- grapes

FISH, MEAT, AND EGGS

- beef
- chicken
- eggs
- pork
- lamb
- fish

DESSERTS

- cake
- pie
- candy
- ice cream
- nuts
- cookies

DRINKS

- milk
- soda
- tea
- orange juice
- coffee

BREAD, RICE, AND SPICES

- bread
- pepper
- salt
- vanilla extract
- mustard
- sugar
- rice
- garlic

A: I like *oranges*.
B: I don't like *ice cream*.

14 Ordinal numbers 📼

1st (first)	7th (seventh)	13th (thirteenth)	19th (nineteenth)	25th (twenty-fifth)
2nd (second)	8th (eighth)	14th (fourteenth)	20th (twentieth)	26th (twenty-sixth)
3rd (third)	9th (ninth)	15th (fifteenth)	21st (twenty-first)	27th (twenty-seventh)
4th (fourth)	10th (tenth)	16th (sixteenth)	22nd (twenty-second)	28th (twenty-eighth)
5th (fifth)	11th (eleventh)	17th (seventeenth)	23rd (twenty-third)	29th (twenty-ninth)
6th (sixth)	12th (twelfth)	18th (eighteenth)	24th (twenty-fourth)	30th (thirtieth)
				31st (thirty-first)

REGISTRATION

A: **Who's** *first*?
B: *Pierre* **is** *first*.

A: **Who's** *fifth*?
B: *I don't know.*

UNIT 1

LESSON 1

What's your name?

Look at the picture. Then listen as you read the conversation. 📼

Lucy:	Hello. My name's Lucy.
Tetsuo:	Hi. I'm Tetsuo.
Lucy:	Where are you from?
Tetsuo:	Japan. And you?
Lucy:	I'm from Mexico.

EXERCISE 1

Practice the conversation. Use your own information. 🔲

A: **Hello. My name's** *Lucy.*
B: **Hi. I'm** *Tetsuo.*

EXERCISE 2

Practice the conversation. Use your own information. 🔲

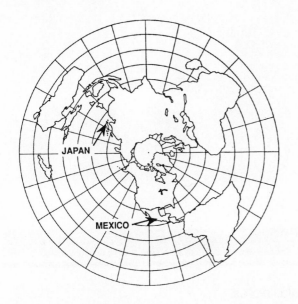

A: **Where are you from?**
B: *Japan.* **And you?**
A: **I'm from** *Mexico.*

EXERCISE 3

Complete the sentences with *'m (am), 's (is),* or *are*. Then listen to the conversation. 🔲

Carlos: Hi. I **'m** Carlos.
  Lynn: Hi. My name ¹_____ Lynn.
Carlos: Where ²_____ you from?
  Lynn: China. And you?
Carlos: I ³_____ from Colombia.

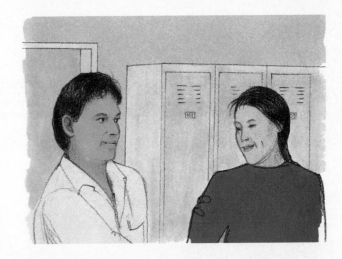

EXERCISE 4

Review the alphabet on page 2. Then spell the words. 🔲

A: **Spell** *English.*
B: *E-n-g-l-i-s-h.*

name   lesson   conversation
read   exercise   review   alphabet
word   write   listen

Listen for the missing words. 📼

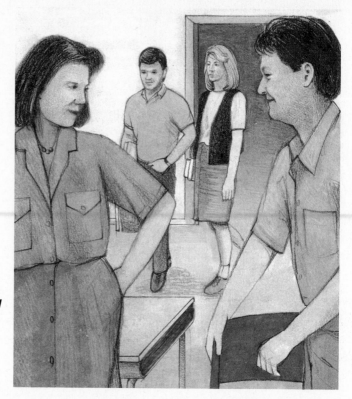

Mrs. Brennan:	Good evening. ***What's*** your ¹___ , please?
Carlos:	²___ Perez.
Mrs. Brennan:	Could you ³___ your last name, please?
Carlos:	⁴_____ .
Mrs. Brennan:	And ⁵___ are you ⁶___ ?
Carlos:	I'm ⁷___ Colombia.
Mrs. Brennan:	Thank you. Please sit down.

Now practice the conversation. Use *Good morning, Good afternoon,* or *Good evening* and your own information.

Talk to three classmates. Ask these questions and take notes.

What's your first (last) name?
Where are you from?
Could you spell that, please?

	First Name	Last Name	Country
1.	_____	_____	_____
2.	_____	_____	_____
3.	_____	_____	_____

Work with a partner. Match the sentences with the responses.

1. Hi. My name's Lynn. ___*c*___   a. Colombia.
2. Could you spell that? ____   b. Carlos.
3. Where are you from? ____   c. Hi. I'm Lucy.
4. What's your first name? ____   d. My last name's Perez.
5. What's your last name? ____   e. P-e-r-e-z.

LESSON 2 This is Keiko.

Look at the picture. Then listen as you read the conversation.

Pierre: Hi, Lucy. How are you?
Lucy: Fine, thanks. And you?
Pierre: Fine. Lucy, this is Keiko. She's a new student. She's from Japan.
Lucy: It's nice to meet you, Keiko.
Keiko: Nice to meet you, too.

Practice the conversation. Use your own information.

A: **Hi,** *Lucy.* **How are you?**
B: **I'm fine, thanks. And you?**
A: **Fine.**

Practice the conversation with two classmates. Use your own information.

A: *Lucy,* **this is** *Keiko.* **She's from** *Japan.*
B: **It's nice to meet you,** *Keiko.*
C: **Nice to meet you, too.**

Ask and answer questions about these people.

Lynn Wang

Carlos Perez

Keiko and Tetsuo

A: **Where is she** from?
B: **She's** from China.

A: **Where is he** from?
B: **He's** from Colombia.

A: **Where are they** from?
B: **They're** from Japan.

1. Pierre Blanc

2. Ann Brennan

3. Gina Poggi

4. Oscar Garcia

5. Pravit Soongwang

6. Yon Mi Lee

7. Marco Martinez and Lucy Mendoza

8. Tony Silva

20 UNIT 1

Work with two classmates. Ask and answer questions.

A: **Where are you from?**
B: **We're from** *Mexico.*

A: **Where are you from?**
B: **I'm from** *China* **and** *Keiko* **is from** *Japan.*

Complete the sentences with *am*, *is*, and *are*. Use contractions (*'m, 's, 're*) when possible.

1. A: Where ＿＿＿ Lynn from?
   B: She ＿＿＿ from China.

2. A: Where ＿＿＿ Keiko and Tetsuo from?
   B: They ＿＿＿ from Japan.

3. A: Where ＿＿＿ Tony from?
   B: He ＿＿＿ from Brazil.

4. A: Where ＿＿＿ you and Lucy from?
   B: We ＿＿＿ from Mexico.

5. A: Where ＿＿＿ you from?
   B: I ＿＿＿ from the United States.

6. A: Where ＿＿＿ Olga from?
   B: She ＿＿＿ from Chile.

Now listen to the conversations. ▭

Listen and choose the correct response. ▭

1. a. He's from China.
   b. She's from China.

2. a. They're from Brazil.
   b. We're from Brazil.

3. a. I'm from Japan.
   b. You're from Japan.

4. a. He's from the United States.
   b. She's from the United States.

5. a. We're from Thailand.
   b. You're from Thailand.

6. a. She's from Canada.
   b. He's from Canada.

7. a. He's from Mexico.
   b. They're from Mexico.

8. a. You're from the United States.
   b. We're from the United States.

Now practice the pronunciation of each pair of sentences. ▭

What about you?

Read the newspaper article. Then do the exercise.

COLLEGE JOURNAL

This is Daniel Stein. He's from Los Angeles, California. He's an English teacher in Dallas.

Michio Tanaka is a new student. He's from Osaka, Japan. He's in English 200. Mr. Stein is his teacher.

Silvio and Ana Costa are in English 200, too. They're from Rio de Janeiro, Brazil.

Choose the right answer.

1. His last name is Stein.
   A. Daniel
   B. Michio
   C. Silvio and Ana

2. He's from Japan.
   A. Daniel
   B. Michio
   C. Silvio and Ana

3. He's a teacher.
   A. Daniel
   B. Michio
   C. Silvio and Ana

4. They're from Brazil.
   A. Daniel
   B. Michio
   C. Silvio and Ana

5. He's a new student.
   A. Daniel
   B. Michio
   C. Silvio and Ana

6. They're in English 200, too.
   A. Daniel
   B. Michio
   C. Silvio and Ana

What about you?
What class are you in?

Look at the model. Then make your own identification card.

Identification Card

Please print:

Name: Mr./Mrs./Miss/Ms. _TANAKA_   _MICHIO_
                        Last   First

Country: _JAPAN_

Teacher's Name: _MR. STEIN_   Class: _ENGLISH 200_

Signature: _Michio Tanaka_
             (sign your name)

EXERCISE 3

Listen and write the sentences. 📼

1. _____ ?   3. _____ .   5. _____ ?
2. _____ ?   4. _____ ?   6. _____ ?

Now give a response to each sentence. Use your own information.

EXERCISE 4

Work with a partner and write the conversation. Present the conversation to the class.

Man: _____
Creature: _____
Man: _____
Creature: _____
Man: _____
Creature: _____

EXERCISE 5

Review the vocabulary on page 1. Then say goodbye to a classmate. 📼

A: Goodbye.
B: Bye. See you tomorrow.

GRAMMAR SUMMARY

VOCABULARY

SUBJECT PRONOUNS

Singular	Plural
I	we
you	you
he	they
she	
it	

PRESENT TENSE: *BE*

Information (Wh-) Questions

	are	you	
Where	**is**	he she it	from?
	are	you they	
What	**'s**	your name?	

Statements

I	**am**	
He She It	**is**	from China.
We They	**are**	
My name	**'s**	Carlos.

Contractions

I'm	(I am)	
He's	(he is)	
She's	(She is)	
It's	(It is)	from China.
You're	(You are)	
We're	(We are)	
They're	(They are)	

PREPOSITIONS

He's **from** Los Angeles, California.
He's a teacher **in** Dallas.

---

alphabet
and
conversation
country
creative
English
exercise
his
identification (I.D.) card
lesson
man
my
new
photo
please
signature
space
student
teacher
too
word

VOCABULARY

COUNTRIES

Brazil
Canada
Chile
China
Colombia
Japan
Korea
Mexico
Spain
Thailand
the United States

VERBS

be
listen
meet
print
read
review
sign
sit (down)
spell
write

PREPOSITIONS

from
in

COMMUNICATION SUMMARY

GREETING PEOPLE

Hi.
Hello.
Good morning.
Good afternoon.
Good evening.

INTRODUCING YOURSELF

My name's Carlos.
I'm Tetsuo.

INTRODUCING PEOPLE

Lucy, this is Keiko.
(It's) Nice to meet you.

EXCHANGING PERSONAL INFORMATION

How are you?
  I'm fine thanks.
What's your name?
  My name's Carlos Perez.
Where are you from?
  I'm from Colombia.
What class are you in?
  I'm in English 101.

SAYING GOODBYE

See you tomorrow.
Goodbye.
Bye.

THANKING

Thank you.
Thanks.

ASKING HOW TO SPELL SOMETHING

Could you spell that, please?

UNIT 2

LESSON 1

What's this?

Look at the pictures. Then listen as you read the conversation.

Mrs. Brennan:	OK. Let's begin. What's this?
Lynn:	It's a book.
Mrs. Brennan:	No. It isn't a book. Keiko?
Keiko:	It's a notebook.
Mrs. Brennan:	Right. What's that, Carlos?
Carlos:	That's an umbrella.
Mrs. Brennan:	Good. What are these?
Tony:	They're pens.
Mrs. Brennan:	No. They aren't pens.
Olga:	Those are pencils.
Mrs. Brennan:	I can't hear. Please stand up.
Olga:	Those are pencils.
Mrs. Brennan:	Right.

Review the vocabulary on page 3. Then answer *That's right* or *That's wrong*.

1. **This** is a notebook.

2. **That**'s an English book.

3. **These** are pens.

4. **Those** are chairs.

5. **This** is an umbrella.

6. **Those** are pieces of paper.

Complete the sentences with *a* or *an* if necessary.

This is **an** umbrella.
That's **a** book.
Those are pens.

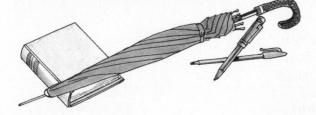

1. That's _____ eraser.
2. These are _____ pieces of chalk.
3. This is _____ desk.
4. That's _____ blackboard.
5. Those are _____ notebooks.
6. This is _____ umbrella.
7. These are _____ English books.
8. Those are _____ erasers.
9. That's _____ wastebasket.
10. These are _____ umbrellas.

Make a sentence about each picture.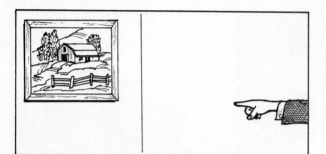

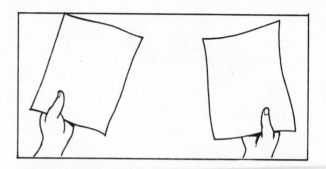

| That's a picture. | These are pieces of paper. |

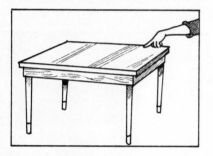

1. . . . table.

2. . . . chairs.

3. . . . briefcases.

4. . . . handbag.

5. . . . students.

6. . . . clock.

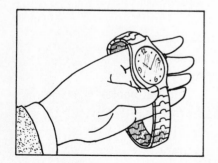

7. . . . watch.

8. . . . teachers.

9. . . . picture.

Ask and answer questions about things in your classroom.

A: What's this (that)?
B: It's *a book.* **(I don't know.)**

B: What are these (those)?
C: They're *books.* **(I don't know.)**

Correct these statements.

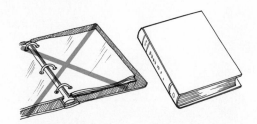

A: This is *a notebook.*
B: No. It isn't *a notebook.* **It's** *a book.*

A: Those are *pens.*
B: No. They aren't *pens.* **They're** *pieces of chalk.*

1. A: That's a picture.
   B: . . .

2. A: These are pieces of chalk.
   B: . . .

3. A: This is an umbrella.
   B: . . .

4. A: Those are pens.
   B: . . .

Listen and choose the correct answer.

1. a. It's a door.
   b. They're doors.

2. a. It's a piece of chalk.
   b. They're pieces of chalk.

3. a. It's an umbrella.
   b. They're umbrellas.

4. a. A notebook.
   b. Notebooks.

5. a. It's a light.
   b. They're lights.

6. a. A window.
   b. Windows.

Now practice the pronunciation of each pair of sentences.

Is this room 322?

Look at the picture. Then listen as you read the conversation.

Roberto: Hi. Are you a new student?

Jim: Yes, I am. Am I late for class?

Roberto: No, you aren't. You're early.

Jim: Is this room 322?

Roberto: No, it isn't. It's room 222.

Jim: Oh. Is this English 601?

Roberto: No, it isn't. It's English 101.

Jim: Oh, excuse me. I'm in the wrong room.

Read the conversation again. Are these sentences True or False?

	T	F
1. Jim is late for class.		
2. Jim is in room 322.		
3. Jim is in English 601.		
4. Roberto is in English 601.		
5. Jim is in the right room.		

Review the numbers on page 6. Then read these numbers.

Course Numbers

1. English 101
2. English 601
3. English 200
4. Math 311

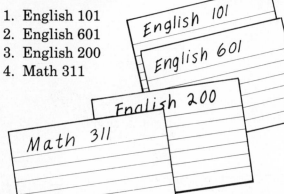

Room Numbers

5. Room 201
6. Room 322
7. Room 1219
8. Room 300

Listen and choose the number you hear.

1. 13	30	5. 17	70
2. 16	60	6. 18	80
3. 15	50	7. 19	90
4. 14	40	8. 12	20

Work with a partner and practice this conversation with your own information.

A: Are you a new student?
B: Yes, I am.
A: Am I late for class?
B: No, you aren't. You're early.
A: Is this room ____ ?
B: No, it isn't. It's room ____ .
A: Oh. Is this English ____ ?
B: No, it isn't! It's English ____ .
A: Oh, excuse me. I'm in the wrong room.

Work with a partner. Ask and answer the questions.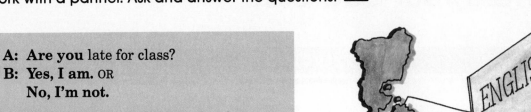

A: **Are you** late for class?
B: **Yes, I am.** OR
   No, I'm not.

A: **Is this** your first English class?
B: **Yes, it is.** OR
   No, it isn't.

A: **Is she** a good teacher?
B: **Yes, she is.** OR
   No, she isn't.

A: **Are your classmates** from Dallas?
B: **Yes, they are.** OR
   No, they aren't.

1. Are you from Japan?
2. Are your classmates from Mexico?
3. Is this an English class?
4. Is this English 110?
5. Are you a teacher?
6. Are you and your partner students?
7. Is this room 200?
8. Is your teacher from the United States?

Ask your own question.
   A: _____ ?
   B: _____ .

What's your address?

EXERCISE 1

Read these numbers.

Area Codes and
Telephone Numbers

1. 555–8022
2. 555–7070
3. (803) 555–4321
4. (214) 555-4353

Zip Codes

5. 10023
6. 94118
7. 60657
8. 75214

	Address	Telephone	C
○	NAME *Alison Cruz*	(214) 555-4353	
	6215 University Street		
	Dallas, Texas 75214		
	NAME		
○	NAME		

Course Numbers	*Room Numbers*	*Addresses*	*Years*
9. English 101	12. Room 304	15. 709 University Street	18. 1801
10. Math 211	13. Room 1011	16. 6215 University Street	19. 1992
11. English 100	14. Room 400	17. 300 University Street	20. 1900

EXERCISE 2

Listen and complete the conversation.

Secretary: ¹____ your name?
   Mike: Mike Murphy.
Secretary: What's your address?
   Mike: ²____ Water Avenue, Dallas, Texas
       ³____.
Secretary: And your telephone number?
   Mike: (214) ⁴____.
Secretary: Your place and year of birth?
   Mike: Denver, Colorado. ⁵____.
Secretary: Thank you.
   Mike: You're welcome.

Look at the conversation in exercise 2 and complete Mike's registration form.

Registration Form

Murphy

| Last Name | First Name |

| Year of Birth | Place of Birth |

| No. | Street |

| City | State | Zip Code |

( )
Area Code   Telephone | Signature |

Complete your own registration form.

Registration Form

| Last Name | First Name |

| Year of Birth | Place of Birth |

| No. | Street |

| City | State | Zip Code |

( )
Area Code   Telephone | Signature |

Ask three classmates their names, addresses, and telephone numbers. Make an address book.

What's your name?
What's your address?
What's your telephone number?

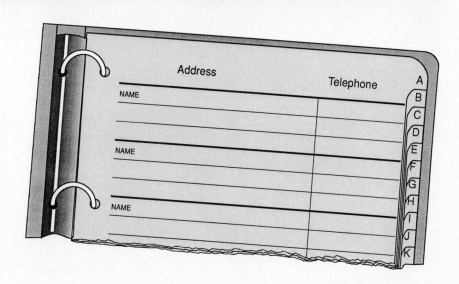

Address | Telephone

NAME

NAME

NAME

A B C D E F G H I J K

DEMONSTRATIVES

What's **this** (**that**)? That (**this**) is an umbrella.
What are **these** (**those**)? **Those** (**these**) are pens.

INDEFINITE ARTICLE *A (AN)*

That's **a** pen.
That's **an** eraser

SINGULAR AND PLURAL NOUNS

A pen → pens
An eraser → erasers

PRESENT TENSE: *BE*

Information (Wh-) Questions

What	's	this?
	are	these?

Affirmative Statements

It	's	a pen.
They	're	chairs.

Negative Statements

It	's	not	a pen.
They	're		desks.

OR

It	isn't	a pencil.
They	aren't	desks.

Yes/No Questions

Am	I	
Are	you	
Is	he she it	in room 322?
Are	we you they	

Short Answers

	you are.	
	I am.	
Yes,	he she it	is.
	you we they	are.

	you aren't.	
	I'm not.	
No,	he she it	isn't.
	you we they	aren't.

a (an)
address
avenue
course
early
false
for
handbag
late
number
registration form
room
street
statement
telephone number
true
umbrella
zip code

I can't hear.
I don't know.
Let's begin.
Please stand up.
Oh.
OK.
place of birth
year of birth
yes/no

VOCABULARY

THE CLASSROOM

blackboard
book
briefcase
chair
classmate
clock
desk
door
eraser
light
math
notebook
partner
pen
pencil
picture
piece of chalk
piece of paper
table
wastebasket
watch
window

CARDINAL NUMBERS

1–1,000 (see page 6)

VERBS

hear
stand (up)

COMMUNICATION SUMMARY

IDENTIFYING OBJECTS

This is an umbrella.
That's a book.
These are pens.
Those are pencils.

ASKING FOR NAMES OF OBJECTS

What's this (that)?
It's a book.
What are these (those)?
They're notebooks.

CORRECTING

It isn't a briefcase. It's a handbag.

CONFIRMING

That's right.
That's wrong.
Good.

EXCHANGING PERSONAL INFORMATION

Are you a new student?
What's your name?
What's your address?
What's your telephone number?

ASKING ABOUT CLASS

Am I late?
Is this room 322?
Is this English 601?

THANKING

Thank you.
You're welcome.

APOLOGIZING

Excuse me. I'm in the wrong room.

Is this your family?

Look at the picture. Then listen as you read the conversation.

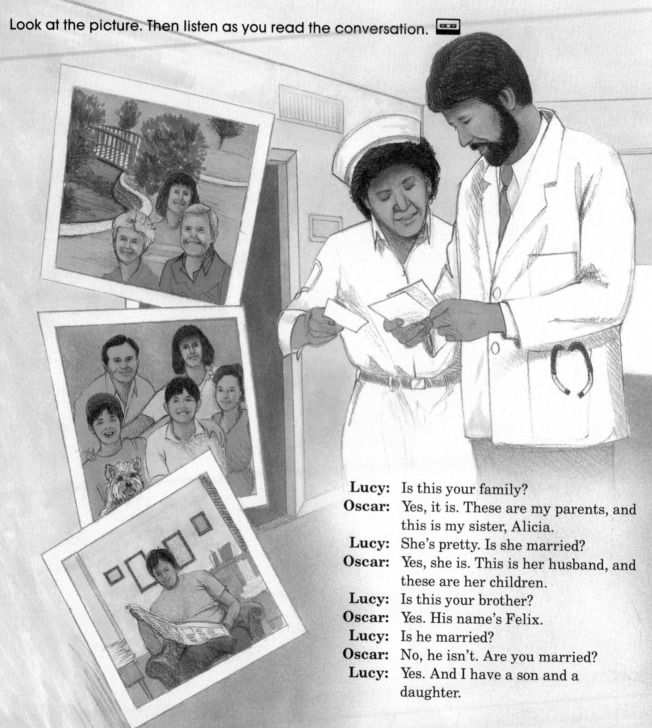

Lucy: Is this your family?

Oscar: Yes, it is. These are my parents, and this is my sister, Alicia.

Lucy: She's pretty. Is she married?

Oscar: Yes, she is. This is her husband, and these are her children.

Lucy: Is this your brother?

Oscar: Yes. His name's Felix.

Lucy: Is he married?

Oscar: No, he isn't. Are you married?

Lucy: Yes. And I have a son and a daughter.

Review the vocabulary on page 12. Then look at the picture of Alicia's family.
Choose the correct word in each sentence.

1. This is my (wife/husband), George.
2. This is my (mother/father), Victor.
3. This is my (mother/father), Gloria.
4. These are my (sons/daughters), Ricardo and Ramon.
5. This is my (son/daughter), Marta.
6. This is my (dog/cat), Coconut.

Complete the sentences with *my, his, her, its, our,* and *their.* Then listen and check your answers.

What's **your** name?
My name is Alicia.
This is my husband. **His** name is George.
This is my daughter. **Her** name is Marta.

These are my sons. **Their** names are Ricardo and Ramon.
Our last name is Castro.
This is my dog. **Its** name is Coconut.

1. Hello. _____ last name is Delgado.

2. _____ name is Olga.

3. And this is my husband. _____ name is Hector.

4. This is my daughter. _____ name is Isabel.

5. These are my sons. _____ names are Eddie and Tommy.

6. This is their cat. _____ name is Tex.

Look at the chart and ask questions.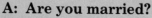

Name	Married	Single
1. Lucy	✔	
2. Pierre		✔
3. Ann and Jerry	✔	
4. Keiko		✔
5. Oscar		✔
6. Gina and Frank		✔
7. Pravit	✔	
8. Lynn		✔
9. Olga and Hector	✔	

A: Is *Lucy* **married?**
B: **Yes, she is.**

A: Is *Pierre* **married?**
B: **No, he isn't.**

A: Are *Ann and Jerry* **married?**
B: **Yes, they are.**

Find out about your classmates.

A: **Are you married?**
B: **Yes, I am.**
A: **Do you have any children?**
B: **Yes. I have** *a son and a daughter.* **(No.)**

A: **Are you married?**
B: **No, I'm not.**
A: **Do you have any brothers and sisters?**
B: **Yes. I have** *two sisters.* **(No.)**

Look at Ann Brennan's family on page 12. Then make a family tree.
Write the names of the people in your family in the boxes.

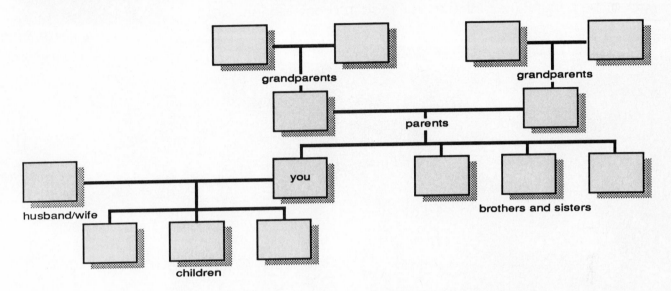

Now tell a classmate who the people are in your family. Follow the examples below.

This is my grandfather. His name's Henry Arden.
These are my children. Their names are Alan and Lisa.

EXERCISE 6

Work with a partner. Look at your partner's family tree and ask questions. 📼

A: **Is that your** *sister*?
B: **Yes, it is. (No, it isn't. It's my** *daughter*.)

A: **Are those your** *children*?
B: **Yes, they are. (No, they aren't. They're my** *grandchildren*.)

EXERCISE 7

Listen to the sentences. Choose the letter of the sentence you hear. 📼

1. a. Is this your mother?
   b. Is this your brother?

2. a. Yes, it is.
   b. Yes, she is.

3. a. Is she married?
   b. Is he married?

4. a. Yes, he is.
   b. Yes, she is.

5. a. Are those his children?
   b. Are those her children?

6. a. Yes, they are.
   b. Yes, we are.

7. a. And is your sister married?
   b. And is her sister married?

8. a. No, she isn't.
   b. No, he isn't.

Now practice the pronunciation of each pair of sentences. 📼

Who's that?

Look at the picture. Then listen as you read the conversation.

Ann: Gina, is this your sweater?
Gina: No. It's Lynn's.

Jerry: Who's that?
Ann: That's Gina Poggi. She's Italian.
Jerry: What?
Ann: She's from Italy.
Jerry: Oh. She's pretty.
Ann: Yes. She has a beautiful smile.
Jerry: What's her occupation?
Ann: She's a bookkeeper.

Review the vocabulary on page 10. Then talk about possessions.

> This (that) is **my** handbag.
> This (that) is Gina**'s** sweater.
> These (those) are Oscar**'s** glasses.

backpack

pen

notebook

bracelet

earrings

jacket

necklace

ring

handbag

wallet

money

glasses

watch

Work with a group. Ask questions about things in the classroom. ▱▱▱

> **A: Excuse me. Is this your** *handbag*?
> **B: No. It's** *Lucy's.* **(Yes, it is. Thank you.)**
>
> **A: Excuse me. Are these your** *papers*?
> **B: No. They're** *Pravit's.* **(Yes, they are. Thank you.)**

Listen and match the people with the things. ▱▱▱

1. Lucy
2. Tony
3. Gina
4. Mrs. Brennan
5. Lynn
6. Carlos
7. Olga
8. Tetsuo

a. glasses
b. English book
c. handbag
d. gloves
e. money
f. briefcase
g. wallet
h. earrings

Look at the chart and practice the conversation.

Lucy   Carlos   Olga   Gina   Tony   Keiko   Oscar   Lynn

A: Who's that?
B: That's *Gina Poggi.* **She's** *Italian.*
A: Excuse me?
B: *She's* **from** *Italy.*
A: Oh.

Name	Nationality	Country
Abe, Keiko	Japanese	Japan
Delgado, Olga	Chilean	Chile
Garcia, Oscar	Spanish	Spain
Mendoza, Lucy	Mexican	Mexico
Perez, Carlos	Colombian	Colombia
Poggi, Gina	Italian	Italy
Silva, Tony	Brazilian	Brazil
Wang, Lynn	Chinese	China

Find out about your classmates.

A: What nationality are you?
B: What?
A: Where are you from?
B: Oh. I'm *American.*

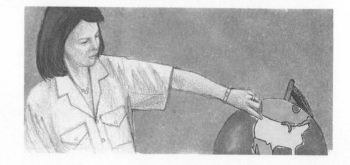

What are the occupations of the students in English 101? Review the vocabulary on page 5 and find out. Then ask questions and complete the chart. 📼

A: **What's** *Keiko***'s occupation?**
B: *She's a secretary.*

Name	Country	Nationality	Age	Occupation
Abe, Keiko	Japan	Japanese	19	secretary
Blanc, Pierre	Canada	Canadian	32	_____
Delgado, Olga	Chile	Chilean	40	housewife
Garcia, Oscar	Spain	Spanish	31	doctor
Lee, Yon Mi	Korea	Korean	25	
Martinez, Marco	Mexico	Mexican	50	security guard
Matsumoto, Tetsuo	Japan	Japanese	35	music teacher
Mendoza, Lucy	Mexico	Mexican	44	
Perez, Carlos	Colombia	Colombian	26	carpenter
Poggi, Gina	Italy	Italian	28	bookkeeper
Rivera, Roberto	Puerto Rico	Puerto Rican	33	
Silva, Tony	Brazil	Brazilian	20	architect
Soongwang, Pravit	Thailand	Thai	35	_____
Wang, Lynn	China	Chinese	21	

How old are the students in English 101? Look at the chart above and ask questions. 📼

A: **How old is** *Keiko***?**
B: *She's 19* (years old).

What about you? How old are you? What's your occupation? Complete the chart with your own information. Then find out about three classmates.

Name	Age	Occupation
you		
1.		
2.		
3.		

New people in town

Read the newspaper article and choose the correct answer.

11 **Wednesday , November 25, 1992** • Dallas Evening News •

NEW PEOPLE IN TOWN

by Roger Muller

Dallas, Texas — Michelle Dubois is French. She is from Nice, France. She is tall and thin. She has long brown hair and blue eyes. Ms. Dubois is 35 years old. She is a doctor.

Ms. Dubois is married. She has a son and daughter. Ms. Dubois and her family aren't in Nice now. They are in Dallas.

1. Ms. Dubois is _____ .
   a. American
   b. French
   c. Italian

2. She is _____ .
   a. short
   b. average height
   c. tall

3. She is _____ .
   a. fat
   b. average weight
   c. thin

4. She has _____ .
   a. long brown hair
   b. short brown hair
   c. long blond hair

5. She has _____ .
   a. brown eyes
   b. blue eyes
   c. green eyes

6. She has _____ .
   a. two sisters
   b. two brothers
   c. two children

Listen and fill in the information.

Name	Roger	Ed	Pamela	Maria	Julie
Nationality	American				
Occupation	reporter				
Age	35				
Height	average				
Hair Color	brown				

Review the vocabulary on page 13. Then describe the people. Listen to the example.

Bill Cosby

Michael Chang

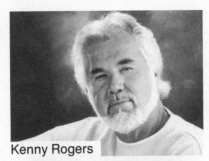

Kenny Rogers

Diana, Princess of Wales

Michelle Pfeiffer

Arnold Schwarzenegger
Danny DeVito

Eddie Murphy

Barbara Bush

Gloria Estefan

Bill Cosby has black hair. He has glasses.

What about you?

I'm _____ .

I have _____ .

Use the newspaper article in exercise 1 as a model. Answer the questions and write a personal description. Indent each paragraph.

Paragraph 1
a. What's your nationality?
b. What city and country are you from?
c. Are you tall, short, or average height?
d. Describe your hair and your eyes.
e. What's your occupation?

Paragraph 2
a. Are you married?
b. Do you have any children or brothers and sisters?
c. Are you and your family in the United States now?
d. What city are you and your family in?

POSSESSIVE ADJECTIVES

What's **your** name?
My name's Alicia.
His name's George.
Her name's Marta.
Its name's Coconut.
Our last name is Castro.
Their names are Ricardo and Ramon.

POSSESSIVE 'S

This is Gina**'s** sweater.
It's Gina**'s**.
What's Keiko**'s** occupation?

PRESENT TENSE: *BE*

Information (Wh-) Questions

Who's that?	That's Gina.
What nationality is she?	She's Italian.
How old is she?	She's 28.

Negative Statements

I	'm not	
He She	isn't	in France now.
We You They	aren't	

PRESENT TENSE: *HAVE*

I	have	
He She It	has	green eyes.
We You They	have	

ADJECTIVES

She is **pretty**.
She has **blue** eyes.
She has a **beautiful** smile.

FAMILY

brother, sister
child (children)
daughter, son
father, mother
grandchildren
grandfather/mother
husband, wife
parents

NATIONALITY

American
Brazilian
Canadian
Chilean
Chinese
Colombian
Italian
Japanese
Korean
Mexican
Puerto Rican
Spanish
Thai

OCCUPATIONS

architect
bookkeeper
carpenter
computer programmer
doctor
housewife
mechanic
music teacher
nurse
photographer
reporter
secretary
security guard
waiter

VOCABULARY

PHYSICAL CHARACTERISTICS

average height
average weight
fat
short
tall
thin

black/blond/brown hair
blue/brown/green eyes

beard
glasses
mustache
smile

beautiful
handsome
pretty

VERB

have

PREPOSITION

by

OTHER

age
at night
bag
cat
color
earrings
first
gloves
jacket
long
married
money
now
or
single
sweater
town
wallet

COMMUNICATION SUMMARY

IDENTIFYING PEOPLE

Who's that?
   That's Gina Poggi.
Is that your father?
   Yes, it is. (No, it isn't.)

This is my brother.
His name is Felix.

DESCRIBING PEOPLE

Roger is average height.
He has brown hair and green eyes.

EXCHANGING PERSONAL INFORMATION

What's your nationality?
   I'm American.
What's your occupation?
   I'm a teacher.
How old are you?
   I'm 35.
Are you married?
   Yes, I am.
Do you have any children?
   Yes. I have a son.

EXCHANGING INFORMATION ABOUT OTHER PEOPLE

Where's she from?
   She's from Italy.
What's her nationality?
   She's Italian.
What's her occupation?
   She's a bookkeeper.
How old is she?
   She's 28.
Is she married?
   No, she isn't.

GETTING SOMEONE'S ATTENTION

Excuse me.

ASKING SOMEONE TO REPEAT

Excuse me?
What?

TALKING ABOUT POSSESSIONS

Is this your handbag?
   No. It's Lucy's.
   Yes, it is. Thank you.
This is my sweater.
These are Oscar's glasses.

LESSON
1

Where's my baseball bat?

Look at the picture. Then listen as you read the conversation.

closet

wall

stereo

bookcase

drawer

baseball

baseball bat

chest

T-shirt

floor

bed

shoes

Eddie: Where's my baseball bat?
Olga: It's on your bed.
Eddie: No, it isn't.
Olga: Well, is it under your bed?
Eddie: No.
Olga: Maybe it's in the closet.
Eddie: No. It isn't in the closet.
Olga: Is it between the desk and the bookcase?
Eddie: No.
Olga: Well, I don't know. Maybe it's next to your chest.
Eddie: Oh, that's right!

EXERCISE 1

Look at the picture on page 50 and describe Eddie Delgado's bedroom. 🔲

> **There's** a bed in Eddie's bedroom.
> **There are** books in Eddie's bedroom.

1. a desk
2. chairs
3. a chest
4. a closet
5. shoes
6. pictures
7. a bookcase
8. clothes
9. a baseball bat
10. a stereo

EXERCISE 2

Look at numbers 2, 5, 6, and 8 in exercise 1 again. Make sentences with *some*. 🔲

> There are **some** books in Eddie's bedroom.

2. chairs
5. shoes
6. pictures
8. clothes

Now make sentences about the things in your classroom.

EXERCISE 3

Look at the picture on page 50 and answer the questions. Then listen and check your answers. 🔲

> A: Is Eddie's jacket **on** the bed or **under** the bed?
> B: It's **on** the bed.
> A: And where are his shoes?
> B: They're **under** the bed.

1. A: Is Eddie's cat **in** the drawer or **in** the closet?
   B: _____ .
   A: And where is his baseball?
   B: _____ .

2. A: Is Eddie's bag **between** the desk and the bookcase or **next to** the chest?
   B: _____ .
   A: And where is his bat?
   B: _____ .

3. A: Are Eddie's pictures **on** the wall or **on** the floor?
   B: _____ .
   A: And where is his T-shirt?
   B: _____ .

in

on

under

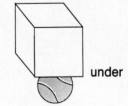

next to

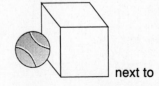

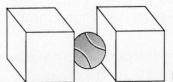

between

Review the vocabulary on page 11. Then complete the sentences with *in, on, under, between,* and *next to.*

The Delgados' kitchen is small. There are a sink and a refrigerator in the kitchen. There is a stove [1]____ the sink and the refrigerator. There is a closet [2]____ the refrigerator. There is a wastebasket [3]____ the sink. There are some cupboards [4]____ the window. There are curtains [5]____ the window.

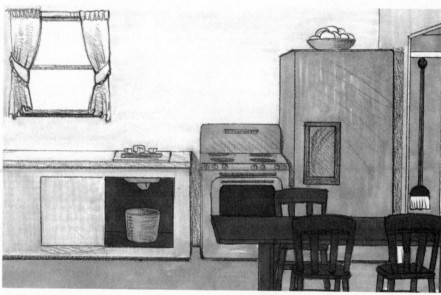

The living room is big. There is a sofa [6]____ the doors. There are two pictures over the sofa, and there is a table in front of the sofa. There are some flowers [7]____ the table. There is a chair [8]____ the corner. There is a lamp behind the chair, and there is a television [9]____ the chair. There is a desk [10]____ the room, too. It is [11]____ the bookcases. There is a dog [12]____ the desk. There is a stereo [13]____ one bookcase. There is a rug [14]____ the floor.

Find these sentences in paragraph 2. What are the three new prepositions?

There are two pictures ____ the sofa, and there is a table ____ the sofa.
There is a lamp ____ the chair. . . .

Look at the picture. Then complete the paragraph with *a* (*an*) or *the*.

This is **a** house.
The house is Olga's.

There is **a** dining room in Olga's house.
The dining room is nice.

There is ¹____ table in ²____ dining room. ³____ table is big. There are four chairs. ⁴____ chairs are around ⁵____ table. There are some pictures on the wall. ⁶____ pictures are small. There is ⁷____ light on the ceiling. ⁸____ light is beautiful.

What is it and where is it? Listen and complete the sentences. 🔲

1. The ____ is ____ the two doors.
2. There's a ____ ____ the two windows.
3. There's a ____ ____ the sofa.
4. There's a ____ ____ the table.
5. There's a ____ ____ the sofa.
6. There's a small ____ ____ the sofa.
7. There's a ____ ____ the chair.
8. There's a ____ ____ the rug.

Now draw a picture of the room.

Draw a room in your house or apartment. Then describe the room to your group. Follow the examples below.

This is my living room.
There's a sofa in front of the window.
There's a table next to the sofa.
There are some pictures on the walls.

LESSON 2

Is there a TV in the bag?

Look at this picture of the Delgados' living room. Then look at the picture on page 52.
Are the pictures the same or different?

Say what is different about the picture.

> **There isn't a** *television in the room.*
> **There aren't any** *pictures on the walls.*

1. rug under the table
2. clock on the bookcase
3. curtains on the windows
4. picture on the desk
5. lamps in the room
6. Is anything else different?

Complete the paragraph with *a*, *some*, and *any*.

There's ¹____ sofa in the living room. There are ²____ bookcases in the room. There are ³____ chairs and a desk in the room. There aren't ⁴____ lamps in the room. There isn't ⁵____ TV in the room. There aren't ⁶____ pictures in the room. There's ⁷____ window in the room. There aren't ⁸____ curtains on the window.

EXERCISE 2

There are two burglars in the Delgados' kitchen. What's in their bag? Look at the picture on page 54 and ask and answer questions. 🔲

A: **Is there a** *TV* **in the bag?**
B: **Yes, there is. (No, there isn't.)**

C: **Are there any** *flowers* **in the bag?**
D: **No, there aren't. (Yes, there are.)**

The burglars are in Eddie's bedroom now. Listen and complete their conversation. 🔲

Joe: Sssssshhh! Be quiet!

Moe: ¹_____ ?

Joe: No, there isn't.

Moe: Oh. Well, ²_____ ?

Joe: Yes, there is.

Moe: Good. ³_____ ?

Joe: Yes, there are.

Moe: ⁴_____ ?

Joe: A baseball bat?

Moe: Yeah. A baseball bat. ⁵_____ .

Work with a partner. Ask about the furniture in your partner's house. Then ask how many there are of each thing. Make a list. 🔲

A: Are there any *chairs in your living room*?

B: Yes, there are.

A: How many are there?

B: There are *four*.

A: Are there any *chairs in your bedroom*?

B: No, there aren't.

Furniture	Living Room	Bedroom	Kitchen
chairs	4		
pictures			
televisions			
tables			
windows			
lamps			
anything else?			

What's the date today?

Review the numbers on page 15.
Then look at the calendars.
Ask about the months of the
year.

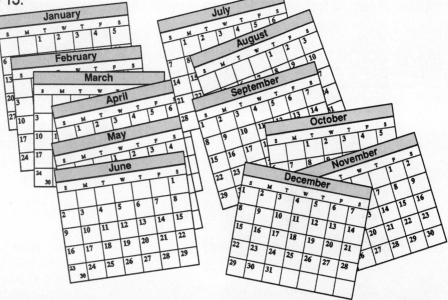

> **A:** What's the *first*
> month of the year?
> **B:** *January.*

Point to the calendar and ask about the date.

> **A:** What the date today?
> **B:** It's *October 10 (tenth).*

Talk to three classmates.
List their names and birthdays.

	Name **Gina**	*Birthday* **July 22**
1.		
2.		
3.		

> **A:** When's your birthday, *Gina*?
> **B:** (It's) *July 22 (twenty-second).*

Look at the pictures and read the paragraph about Boston, Massachusetts.
Then answer the questions.

FOCUS ON BOSTON

Winter   December 21—March 21

Spring   March 21—June 21

There are four seasons in Boston. They are winter, spring, summer, and fall. The weather in winter is cold and snowy. The weather in spring is windy and rainy. The weather in summer is hot and sunny. The weather in fall is cloudy and cool, but there isn't any snow.

Summer   June 21—September 21

Fall   September 21—December 21

1. How many seasons are there in Boston?
2. What are the seasons?
3. What's the weather like in winter?

4. What's the weather like in spring?
5. What's the weather like in summer?
6. What's the weather like in fall?

Now ask your partner questions about the seasons in his or her city.

Ask and answer questions about the weather.

> **A:** What's the weather like?
> **B:** It's *hot*.

Listen and complete this postcard.

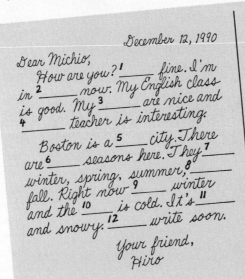

December 12, 1990

Dear Michio,
How are you? ¹_____ fine. I'm
in ²_____ now. My English class
is good. My ³_____ are nice and
⁴_____ teacher is interesting.
Boston is a ⁵_____ city. There
are ⁶_____ seasons here. They ⁷_____
winter, spring, summer, ⁸_____
fall. Right now ⁹_____ winter
and the ¹⁰_____ is cold. It's ¹¹_____
and snowy. ¹²_____ write soon.

Your friend,
Hiro

Mr. Michio Tanaka
193 Washington St.
Dallas, Texas 75214

Write a postcard to a friend. Use Hiro's postcard as a model.

1. Use one of these words in your address:
   Miss or *Mrs.* (*Ms.*) or *Mr.*
2. Write the date like this: *December 12, 1990*
3. Write a greeting: *Dear Michio,*
4. In paragraph one, write about your English
   class.
5. In paragraph two, write about the weather
   in your city.
6. Write a closing: *Your friend,* or *Love,*
7. Sign your name: *Hiro*

PREPOSITIONS OF PLACE

The picture is	**in** **on** **under** **over** **next to** **behind** **in front of**	the desk.
The chairs are	**between** **around**	the bookcases. the table.

THERE IS/ARE

Affirmative Statements

There	**'s**	a television in the room.
	are	(some) pictures on the wall.

Negative Statements

There	**isn't**	a television in the room.
	aren't	(any) pictures on the wall.

Yes/No Questions

Is	there	a TV in the bag?
Are		(any) flowers in the bag?

Short Answers

Yes, **there is.**	No, **there isn't.**
Yes, **there are.**	No, **there aren't.**

PRESENT TENSE: *BE*

Information (Wh-) Questions

When is your birthday? It's July 22.
How many (chairs) are there? There are four.

Questions with Or

Is Eddie's jacket on the bed **or** under the bed? It's on the bed.

SOME AND *ANY* WITH COUNT NOUNS

There are **some** pictures on the wall.
There are**n't any** pictures on the wall.

DEFINITE ARTICLE: *THE*

This is a dining room. There is a table in **the** dining room. **The** table is big.

VOCABULARY

baseball
baseball bat
big
birthday
but
clothes
corner
flower
focus
interesting
nice
shoes
small
T-shirt

Be quiet!
Dear . . .
Love,/Your friend,
Miss, Mrs., Mr., Ms.
Please write soon.
right now
Well,
Yeah.

ORDINAL NUMBERS

1st–31st (see page 15)

THE HOUSE AND FURNITURE

bed
bedroom
ceiling
chest
clock
closet
cupboards
curtain
dining room
drawer
floor
kitchen
lamp
living room
refrigerator
rug
sink
sofa
stereo
stove
television (TV)
wall

THE SEASONS

fall
spring
summer
winter

THE WEATHER

cold
cool
hot
rainy
snow
snowy
sunny
windy

THE MONTHS

January
February
March
April
May
June
July
August
September
October
November
December

PREPOSITIONS

around
behind
between
in
in front of
next to
on
over
under

DESCRIBING THINGS AND THEIR LOCATIONS

This is my living room.
There are some pictures on the wall.

DESCRIBING DIFFERENCES

There isn't a stereo in the room.
There aren't any flowers on the table.

TALKING ABOUT QUANTITY

How many (chairs) are there?
    There are four.

ASKING FOR AND GIVING LOCATIONS

Is there a TV in the bag?
    Yes, there is.
Are Eddie's shoes on the bed or under the bed?
    They're under the bed.

TALKING ABOUT THE WEATHER AND THE SEASONS

How many seasons are there?
    There are four seasons.
What's the weather like in summer?
    It's hot and sunny.

ASKING FOR AND GIVING DATES

What's the date today?
    It's October 10, 1991.
When's your birthday?
    It's July 22.

A new apartment

Look at the pictures. Then listen as you read the sentences under each picture.

1. Keiko and Lynn are friends. They are looking for an apartment.

2. Lynn is living with her aunt and uncle in a small apartment. She is unhappy there.

3. Keiko isn't living with her family. She's staying in a small hotel. The hotel is awful.

4. Right now Lynn is reading the apartment ads in the newspaper.

5. And Keiko is calling about an apartment for rent.

6. Now they are looking at an apartment. They are standing in the living room.

Look at the pictures and sentences on page 62. Then choose the correct word in the parentheses in these sentences.

Keiko **is living** in Dallas. She **isn't living** in Japan.
Keiko and Lynn **are studying** English. They **aren't teaching** English.

1. Lynn (is/are) living with her aunt and uncle.
2. Keiko (isn't/aren't) living with her family.
3. She (is/are) staying in a small hotel.
4. Keiko and Lynn (is/are) looking for an apartment.

5. They (isn't/aren't) looking for a house.
6. Lynn (is/are) reading the newspaper.
7. Keiko (is/are) calling about an apartment.
8. They (is/are) standing in the living room of their new apartment.

Make sentences about the pictures. Then listen and check your answers.

Gina is visiting her brother this weekend.

Mr. and Mrs. Brennan are relaxing today.

1. Pierre (work) at the restaurant today.

2. Marco and Carlos (study) at the library now.

3. Roberto (paint) his kitchen this weekend.

4. Yon Mi (not read) the newspaper now.

5. Lucy (not clean) her kitchen right now.

6. Oscar (go) to work today.

What about you?
I'm _____ right now.

UNIT 5   **63**

Look at the pictures in exercise 2. Ask and answer these questions.

> **A:** Is Gina visiting her father this weekend?
> **B:** No, she isn't.
> **A:** Are Mr. and Mrs. Brennan relaxing today?
> **B:** Yes, they are.

1. Is Pierre eating at the restaurant today?
2. Are Marco and Carlos studying at the library now?
3. Is Roberto painting his living room this weekend?
4. Is Yon Mi watching television now?
5. Is Lucy cleaning her kitchen right now?
6. Is Oscar going to work?
7. Is your partner answering your questions?

Work with a group. Ask questions about the picture. Use the words in the list.

1. talk on the telephone
2. knock at the door
3. fight
4. cook
5. bark
6. study

> **A:** Is Eddie talking on the telephone?
> **B:** No, he isn't.

Listen and complete the paragraphs.

Olga ¹____ having a good day. The ²____ is a mess. The ³____ are fighting. ⁴____ dog's barking. A salesman is ⁵____ at the door.

Olga is ⁶____ tired and she's ⁷____ for a babysitter. ⁸____ calling her friends but ⁹____ friends are busy. She ¹⁰____ very happy!

What are you doing?

Olga is talking to Keiko. Look at the picture.
Then listen as you read the conversation.

Keiko:	Hello?
Olga:	Hi, Keiko. This is Olga.
Keiko:	Oh, hi, Olga. How are you?
Olga:	Oh, I'm OK. What are you doing?
Keiko:	I'm studying.
Olga:	Oh. What's Lynn doing?
Keiko:	She's taking pictures for a women's magazine.
Olga:	Oh?
Keiko:	Yeah. There are two models here, and they're wearing beautiful dresses. And what are you doing?
Olga:	I'm looking for a babysitter. I'm going crazy!

Read the conversation on page 65 again. Then answer *That's right*, *That's wrong*, or *I don't know*.

1. Olga is talking to Keiko.
2. Keiko is studying English.
3. Lynn is taking pictures for a newspaper.

4. There are three models in the apartment.
5. The models are wearing dresses.
6. The models are Lynn's friends.

These people are working. What are they doing? Ask and answer questions. Then listen and check your answers.

reporter/write a story
A: What's the reporter **doing?**
B: He's writing a story.
(Note: write → writing)

carpenters/build a house
A: What are the carpenters **doing?**
B: They're building a house.

1. secretary/type a letter

2. nurses/work in a hospital

3. mechanic/fix a car

4. waiters/clean tables

5. English teacher/
   teach a class

6. architects/draw houses

Review the vocabulary on page 10. Then ask and answer questions about the picture.

A: **What's the** *first woman* **wearing?**
B: *She's wearing a skirt and a blouse.*
A: **What color is** *her skirt?*
B: **It's** *red.*

Call your partner on the telephone.

A: **Hello?**
B: **Hi,** *Keiko.* **This is** *Olga.*
A: **Oh, hi,** *Olga.* **How are you?**
B: **I'm** *OK.* **What are you doing?**
A: **I'm** *studying.* **And what are you doing?**
B: **I'm** *looking for a babysitter.*

What about you?
What are you wearing?
What color is it?

Look at these singular and plural nouns.

Nouns ending in -x, -s, -ch, or -sh	Nouns ending in -y	Nouns ending in -f and -fe	Irregular plurals
box **boxes** dress **dresses** watch **watches** dish **dishes**	library **libraries**	scarf **scarves** knife **knives**	child **children** man **men** woman **women**

Now complete these sentences.

> The teacher is wearing **a skirt** and **a blouse**.
> The students are wearing **skirts** and **blouses**, too.

1. The teacher is wearing a scarf.
   The students are wearing _____ , too.

2. The teacher is looking at her watch.
   The students are looking at their _____ , too.

3. The teacher is writing a story.
   The students are writing _____ , too.

4. The teacher has one English class today.
   The students have three English _____ today.

5. The teacher is a woman.
   The students are _____ , too.

Roberto is interviewing Lynn for the school newspaper. Read the questions. Then listen and write the answers. 🔲

1. Where is Lynn from?
2. What is her profession?
3. Is she working in the United States?

4. Is she studying in the United States?
5. What is she studying?
6. Where is she studying?

Is it near the park?

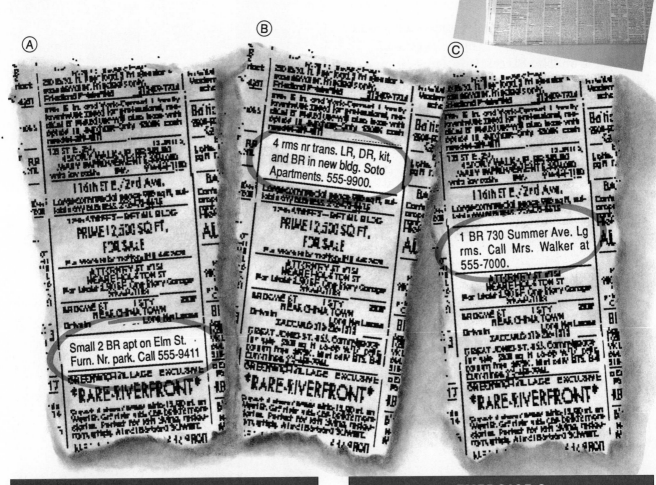

Ⓐ Ⓑ Ⓒ

> Small 2 BR apt on Elm St. Furn. Nr. park. Call 555-9411

> 4 rms nr trans. LR, DR, kit, and BR in new bldg. Soto Apartments. 555-9900.

> 1 BR 730 Summer Ave. Lg rms. Call Mrs. Walker at 555-7000.

EXERCISE 1

Look at the three apartment ads. Match the words with their abbreviations.

1. apartment   __j__   a. nr
2. bedroom   ____   b. trans
3. building   ____   c. St
4. dining room   ____   d. Ave
5. furnished   ____   e. furn
6. large   ____   f. LR
7. near   ____   g. BR
8. rooms   ____   h. bldg
9. transportation   ____   i. lg
10. Street   ____   j. apt
11. living room   ____   k. DR
12. Avenue   ____   l. rms

EXERCISE 2

Match the descriptions with the apartments in exercise 1.

1. There are four rooms.   Apt. __B__
2. It's small.   Apt. ____
3. It's in a new building.   Apt. ____
4. It's furnished.   Apt. ____
5. There's a dining room.   Apt. ____
6. There are two bedrooms.   Apt. ____
7. There are large rooms.   Apt. ____
8. It's near the park.   Apt. ____
9. There's good transportation.   Apt. ____
10. It's on Summer Avenue.   Apt. ____

Read about Silvio and Ana Costa's new neighborhood.

   Silvio and Ana have a new apartment in a wonderful neighborhood. Their apartment building is on Elm Street. It is across from a park. They are happy there.

   There are a supermarket, a drugstore, a post office, a bank, a movie theater, and a police station near their apartment building. The drugstore is on Washington Street. It's between the post office and the police station. The movie theater is on Washington Street. It's across from the bank. The supermarket is on Park Avenue.

   There are a library and a hospital in their neighborhood, too. The hospital is on the corner of Ridge Avenue and Elm Street. It's next to the library.

Now look at the map and write the names of the places. Refer to the reading if necessary.

1. _**hospital**_
2. _____
3. _____
4. _____
5. _____
6. _____

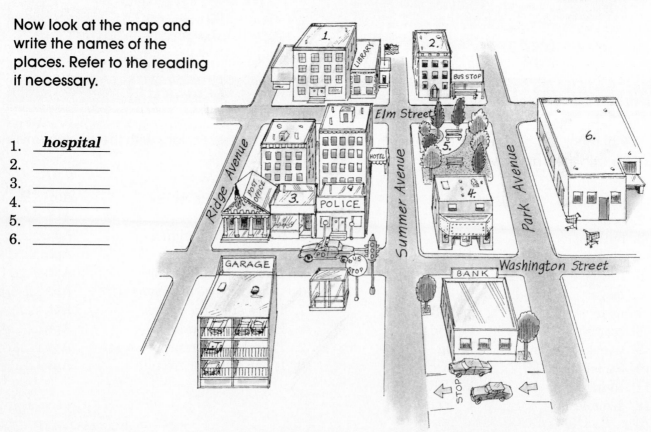

EXERCISE 4

Look at the map in exercise 3. Ask and answer questions.

> **A:** **Excuse me. Where's the** *library*?
> **B:** **It's** *on the corner of Elm Street and Summer Avenue.* **(It's** *next to the hospital.***)**
> **A:** **Thanks a lot. (Thank you.)**

Now ask about places near your school.

EXERCISE 5

Listen to the questions about Ana and Silvio Costa and write the answers.

> Are Silvio and Ana Costa living in Dallas or are they living in Boston?
> **They're living in Dallas.**

1. _____ .
2. _____ .
3. _____ .
4. _____ .
5. _____ .
6. _____ .

EXERCISE 6

Interview the people in your classroom. Find someone who . . .

	Name
1. is studying English.	_____
2. isn't studying English.	_____
3. is wearing black shoes.	_____
4. isn't wearing a watch.	_____
5. is living in an apartment.	_____
6. isn't living in an apartment.	_____
7. is working near your school.	_____
8. isn't having a good day.	_____

PRESENT CONTINUOUS TENSE

Affirmative Statements

I	'm (am)		
He She	's (is)	living	in Dallas.
You We They	're (are)		

Negative Statements

I	'm not (am not)		
He She	isn't (is not)	living	in Dallas.
You We They	aren't (are not)		

Yes/No Questions

Are	you		
Is	he she	living	in Dallas?
Are	they		

Short Answers

	I we	am are.
Yes,	he she	is.
	they	are.

	I we	'm not aren't.
No,	he she	isn't.
	they	aren't.

Information (Wh-) Questions

	are	you	
What	is	he she	studying?
Where	are	they	

English.
At home.

PREPOSITIONS

It's **on the corner of** Elm Street and Summer Avenue.
It's **across from** the park.
They're studying **at** home.
She's going **to** work.

PLURAL NOUNS

Nouns ending in -x, -s, -ch, or -sh	Nouns ending in -y	Nouns ending in -f and -fe	Irregular plurals
box → boxes dress → dresses watch → watches dish → dishes	library → libraries	scarf → scarves knife → knives	child → **children** man → **men** woman → **women**

ad
aunt
awful
babysitter
building
busy
car
dish
furnished
happy
here
knife
large
letter
magazine
man (men)
mess
model
neighborhood
story
subject
television
there
tired
transportation
uncle
unhappy
woman (women)
wonderful
work

for rent
I'm going crazy!
this weekend

COLORS
beige
gray
pink
purple
red
white
yellow

VOCABULARY

CLOTHES

blouse
blue jeans
bracelet
dress
hat
necklace
pants
scarf
skirt
suit
tie
watch

PLACES

bank
drugstore
garage
hospital
hotel
library
movie theater
park
police station
post office
restaurant
school
supermarket

VERBS

bark	paint
build	relax
call	stand
clean	stay
cook	study
do	take
draw	talk
eat	teach
fight	type
fix	visit
go	watch
knock	wear
live	work
look	

COMMUNICATION SUMMARY

TALKING ABOUT THE PRESENT

Are you studying here?
  Yes, I am.
What are you studying?
  I'm studying English.
Where are you studying?
  At the English Language Institute.

TALKING ABOUT CLOTHES AND COLORS

What are you wearing?
  I'm wearing a skirt.
What color is your skirt?
  It's red.

TALKING ON THE TELEPHONE

Hello?
  Hi, Keiko. This is Olga.
Oh, hi, Olga. How are you?
  I'm OK. What are you doing?
I'm studying.

ASKING FOR AND GIVING LOCATIONS

Excuse me. Where's the library?
  It's on the corner of Elm Street and Summer Avenue.
Thanks a lot.

LESSON
1

The Castros' week

Look at the pictures. Then listen as you read the sentences under each picture.

1. Alicia and George Castro work on Monday, Tuesday, Wednesday, Thursday, and Friday.

2. They work in an office.

3. After work, they play tennis or go swimming.

4. Before they go home, they go to the supermarket.

5. Then they cook and eat dinner.

6. After dinner, they watch television.

7. They don't work on the weekend. On Saturday, they clean and do errands.

8. On Sunday, they relax or go to the movies.

Look at the pictures and sentences on page 74. Then choose the correct answer.

1. Alicia and George work
   a. on Monday, Tuesday, Wednesday, Thursday, and Friday.
   b. on Saturday and Sunday.

2. They work
   a. in an office.
   b. at home.

3. They play tennis or go swimming
   a. before work.
   b. after work.

4. Before they go home,
   a. they go to the supermarket.
   b. they go to the movies.

5. After dinner,
   a. they go to the movies.
   b. they watch television.

6. They do errands
   a. on Sunday.
   b. on Saturday.

Work with a group. Point to the calendar and ask about the days of the week. ▭▭

A: **What day is today?**
B: **(It's)** *Monday.*

Now match the abbreviations with the days.

1. Sunday	a. Wed.
2. Tuesday	b. Mon.
3. Saturday	c. Tues.
4. Monday	d. Fri.
5. Thursday	e. Sat.
6. Wednesday	f. Thurs.
7. Friday	g. Sun.

March

Sunday	Monday	Tuesday	Wednesday	Thursday	Friday	Saturday
		1	2	3	4	5
6	7	8	9	10	11	12
13	14	15	16	17	18	19
20	21	22	23	24	25	26
27	28	29	30	31		

Complete the sentences with the verbs in this list:

work   study   visit   go   teach   play   do   watch

We **go** swimming on the weekend.
We **don't go** swimming every day.

1. I ____ my friends on Sunday.
   I ____ my parents.

2. They ____ in a hospital from Monday to Friday.
   They _go_ there on Saturday and Sunday.

3. We ____ errands on Saturday.
   We ____ our homework.

4. You _✗_ English on Tuesday and Thursday.
   You ____ English on Monday and Wednesday.

5. They ____ tennis every day.
   They ____ baseball.

6. I ____ at the library every weekend.
   I ____ at home.

7. They ____ swimming on Saturday.
   They ____ swimming on Sunday.

8. We ____ television on Friday, Saturday, and Sunday.
   We ____ television from Monday to Thursday.

Listen for the missing words.

Ricardo and Ramon are Alicia and George Castro's sons. They go to [1]____ . They are twins [2]____ they are in the same [3]____ .

Ricardo and Ramon [4]____ English, math, and history [5]____ day. They have science on [6]____ and Thursday. They have music [7]____ Tuesday and Thursday, [8]____ .

After school, [9]____ play with their friends and [10]____ their homework. They have dinner with [11]____ parents and sister, and then they [12]____ television.

On Saturday morning, they have [13]____ lessons. On Saturday afternoon, they [14]____ their rooms. On Sunday, they study or [15]____ swimming. Sometimes they go to the [16]____ with their parents.

Read the paragraphs in exercise 4. Then answer the questions.

> **A: Do** Ricardo and Ramon **go** to school?
> **B: Yes, they do.**
>
> **A: Do** they **work?**
> **B: No, they don't.**

1. Do Ricardo and Ramon have history every day?
2. Do they have science every day?
3. Do they have music on Tuesday and Thursday?
4. Do they play with their friends after school?
5. Do they do errands after school?
6. Do they do their homework on Saturday morning?

First answer these questions about yourself. Answer YES or NO. Then ask your partner the questions.

Do you . . .	You	Your Partner
1. go to school?		
2. have English every day?		
3. study French?		
4. have class on Saturday?		
5. do your homework every day?		
6. watch television after dinner?		
7. WRITE YOUR OWN QUESTION.		

LESSON 2 Dear Felix

Felix and Oscar are Alicia's brothers. Listen as you read Alicia's letter to Felix.

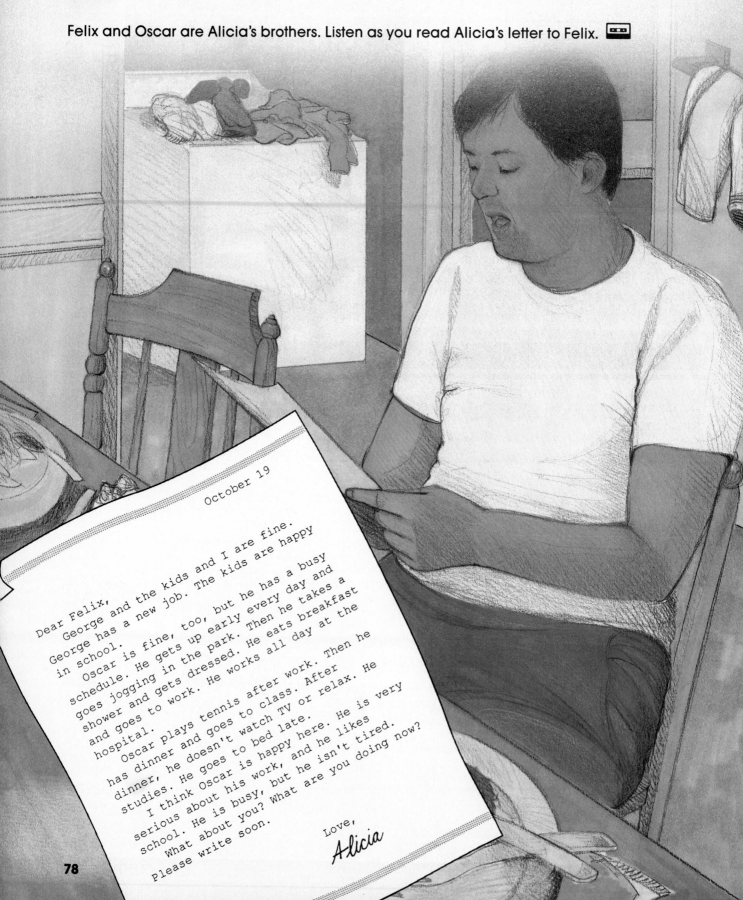

October 19

Dear Felix,

George and the kids and I are fine.
George has a new job. The kids are happy
in school.

Oscar is fine, too, but he has a busy
schedule. He gets up early every day and
goes jogging in the park. Then he takes a
shower and gets dressed. He eats breakfast
and goes to work. He works all day at the
hospital.

Oscar plays tennis after work. Then he
has dinner and goes to class. After
dinner, he doesn't watch TV or relax. He
studies. He goes to bed late.

I think Oscar is happy here. He is very
serious about his work, and he likes
school. He is busy, but he isn't tired.
What about you? What are you doing now?
Please write soon.

Love,
Alicia

78

Read Alicia's letter to Felix again. Then choose the correct picture.

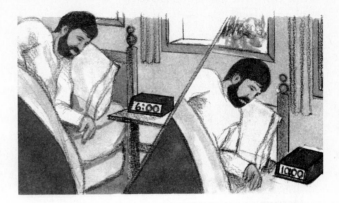

1. a. Oscar has a busy schedule.   b. Oscar doesn't have a busy schedule.

2. a. He gets up early.   b. He gets up late.

3. a. He goes swimming in the park.   b. He goes jogging in the park.

4. a. He takes a shower and gets dressed.   b. He takes a shower and goes to bed.

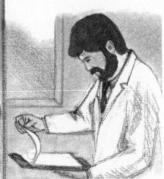

5. a. He works all night.   b. He works all day.

6. a. After class, he watches TV or relaxes.   b. After class, he doesn't watch TV or relax.

What's Felix like? Make sentences about Felix with the phrases below the pictures. 📼

Felix gets up late.
He goes into the bathroom and washes.
He relaxes in bed.
He watches the news.
He studies the schedule of TV movies.

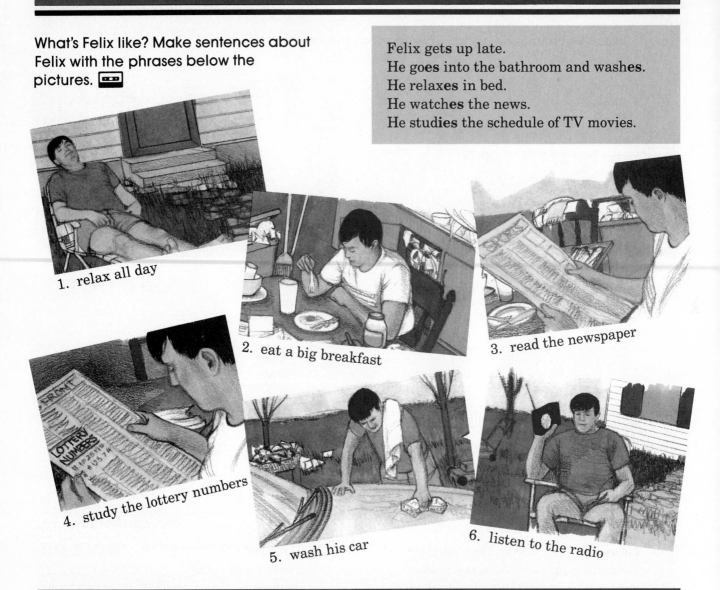

1. relax all day

2. eat a big breakfast

3. read the newspaper

4. study the lottery numbers

5. wash his car

6. listen to the radio

Oscar, Alicia, and Felix are very different. Look at the chart. Talk about Oscar and Alicia and their brother Felix.

Oscar and Alicia get up early, but Felix **doesn't get up** early.
Oscar and Alicia **don't relax** all day, but Felix relaxes all day.

	Oscar	Alicia	Felix
1. get up early	✓	✓	
2. have a job	✓	✓	
3. go to work	✓	✓	
4. work all day	✓	✓	
5. relax all day			✓
6. exercise	✓	✓	
7. do errands	✓	✓	
8. study English	✓	✓	
9. smoke			✓
10. listen to the radio			✓

EXERCISE 4

Look at the chart in exercise 3 and ask questions about Oscar, Alicia, and Felix.

A: Does Oscar *get up early*?	**A: Does Felix** *have a job*?	**A: Do Oscar and Alicia** *exercise*?
B: Yes, he does.	**B: No, he doesn't.**	**B: Yes, they do.**

EXERCISE 5

Alicia is talking to a friend. Listen to the conversation and choose the correct answer.

1. Alicia is talking about
   a. her brothers.
   b. her children.

2. What are their names?
   a. Ricardo, Ramon, and Marta.
   b. Oscar and Felix.

3. Do they live in Dallas?
   a. Yes. They live in Dallas.
   b. Oscar lives in Dallas, but Felix lives in Denver.

4. Are Oscar and Felix the same?
   a. Yes, they are.
   b. No, they're different.

5. What's Oscar like?
   a. He's serious. He works hard and studies a lot.
   b. He's lazy. He stays home and watches TV all day.

6. What's Felix like?
   a. He's serious. He works hard and studies a lot.
   b. He's lazy. He stays home and watches TV all day.

EXERCISE 6

Listen to the conversation in exercise 5 again. Then write your own conversation and present it to the class. Use the ideas below or your own ideas.

A: Do you have any brothers and sisters?
   Do you have any friends in this class?
B: Yes. I have one/two _____ (and _____).

A: Do/does _____ live here in _____ ?
   Do/does _____ live near you?
B: Yes, _____ do/does.
   No. _____ live/lives in _____ .

A: What's _____ like?
B: _____'s very interesting.
   _____'s very nice, but he's lazy.

I think I'm in love.

Listen and write the sentences. 📼

Susan doesn't work on the weekend.

a. _____   d. _____
b. _____   e. _____
c. _____   f. _____

Greg Scott is writing a letter to his sister. Complete his letter with the sentences from exercise 1.

Dear Linda,
    I have a new friend here in Denver.
Her name's Susan Palmer, and she's very
nice. She's a bookkeeper at a hotel. **1** _____.
Her family lives there. She has a brother,
but **2** _____.
    Susan has a very busy schedule. **3** _____
and she studies international business on
Tuesday and Thursday nights. She is serious
about her work **4** _____.
    Susan doesn't work on the weekend. On
Saturday **5** _____. Sometimes Susan and I go
to the movies on Sunday. Sometimes **6** _____
or we play tennis.
    Susan is changing my life. I don't sit
at home all day now. I have a job, and I
exercise every day! I think I'm in love!

        Love,
        Greg

EXERCISE 3

Interview a classmate and take notes. Ask these questions.

1. Could you spell your last name, please?
2. What's your occupation?
3. Where are you from?
4. Are you married?
5. Do you have any brothers and sisters?
6. Do you have a busy schedule?
7. Do you work all day?
8. Do you go to school, too?
9. Do you like your job?
10. Do you work on the weekend?
11. Do you play any sports?
12. Anything else?

EXERCISE 4

Write a letter about a classmate. Use the information in exercise 3.

Paragraph one —use the information from interview questions 1–5.

Paragraph two —use the information from interview questions 6–9.

Paragraph three—use the information from interview questions 10 and 11.

Don't forget —the date, the greeting, the closing, and your signature.

Use the letter in exercise 1 as a model.

EXERCISE 5

Is Greg the same or different? Work with a group and talk about the pictures.

Greg doesn't have a girlfriend in the first picture.
He isn't watching TV in the second picture.

SIMPLE PRESENT TENSE

Affirmative Statements

I You We They	work	every day.
He She (It)	works	

Negative Statements

I You We They	don't (do not)	work	every day.
He She (It)	doesn't (does not)		

Yes/No Questions

Do	you we they	get up	early?
Does	he she (it)		

Short Answers

Yes,	I you they	do.
	he she (it)	does.

No,	I you they	don't.
	he she	doesn't.

PREPOSITIONS

I don't work **on** Sunday.
Do they live **near** you?

CONJUNCTION: *BUT*

Oscar and Alicia have jobs, **but** Felix doesn't have a job.

after
a lot
before
different
girlfriend
hard
international
job
kid
lazy
lesson
life
lottery number
movies
news
office
radio
schedule
serious
sometimes
sport
the same
twins
week

all day/night
Don't forget.
every day/weekend
I'm in love!
on Saturday morning/
    afternoon

DAYS OF THE WEEK

Sunday
Monday
Tuesday
Wednesday
Thursday
Friday
Saturday

VOCABULARY

SCHOOL SUBJECTS

business
French
history
science

MEALS

breakfast
lunch
dinner

VERBS

change
do errands
do *my* homework
exercise
get dressed
get up
go jogging/swimming
go to bed
go to the movies
have class
like
listen to the radio
play
play tennis
smoke
stay home
take a shower
think
wash

PREPOSITION

near

COMMUNICATION SUMMARY

ASKING FOR AND GIVING THE DAY

What day is today?
  (It's) Monday.

TELLING ABOUT YOUR WEEK

I work from Monday to Friday.
I stay home and study on the weekend.

FINDING OUT ABOUT PEOPLE'S SCHEDULES

Do they have science every day?
  No, they don't.
Do you watch TV after dinner?
  Yes, I do.

ASKING ABOUT RELATIVES AND FRIENDS

Do you have any friends in this class?
(Do you have any brothers or sisters?)
  Yes. I have one. Her name's Susan.
Does she live near you.
  Yes, she does.
What's she like?
  She's very serious. She works every day and studies at night.

EXPLAINING DIFFERENCES

Oscar and Alicia have jobs, but Felix doesn't have a job.

UNIT 7

LESSON 1

What time is it?

Yon Mi is going to Houston this weekend. Look at the picture.
Then listen as you read the conversation.

BUS DEPARTUR **T TERM**

ALLAS
UBBOCK
PASO
ENIX

TICKETING

Ticket agent:	Can I help you?
Yon Mi:	Yes. When does the next bus leave for Houston?
Ticket agent:	At 9:00.
Yon Mi:	And what time does it arrive?
Ticket agent:	At 3:00.
Yon Mi:	What time is it now?
Ticket agent:	It's 8:45.
Yon Mi:	Thank you.
Ticket agent:	You're welcome.

Ask the time.

What time is it?
It's 9:00 (nine o'clock).

What time is it?
It's 9:05 (nine-o-five).

What time is it?
It's 9:10 (nine-ten).

1.   2.   3.   4.   5.

6.   7.   8.   9.   10.

Yon Mi is a computer programmer. Look at the pictures and correct the sentences.

Yon Mi works for a small company.

She doesn't work for a small company. She works for a large company.

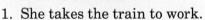

1. She takes the train to work.

2. She gets to her office at 8:00.

3. She stands in front of her computer at 9:00, and her day begins.

4. At 12:00, Yon Mi and her friends eat breakfast in the cafeteria.

5. They finish work at 9:00.

UNIT 7   **87**

EXERCISE 3

First, complete the question with *do* or *does*. Then ask and answer the questions about Yon Mi. 📼

> A: **What does** Yon Mi **do** for a living?
> B: She's a computer programmer.
>
> A: **Where do** Yon Mi and her friend **eat** lunch?
> B: They eat in the cafeteria.

1. How _____ Yon Mi go to work?
2. What time _____ she get to her office?
3. What time _____ Yon Mi and her friend eat lunch?
4. When _____ they finish work?

EXERCISE 4

Work with a partner. Practice the conversation with your own information.

A: What do you do for a living?
B: _____ . (I'm not working right now. I'm a student.)
A: Where do you work/go to school?
B: _____ .
A: How do you go to work/school?
B: I take a bus/train/taxi. (I walk/drive.)
A: What time do you get to work/school?
B: _____ .
A: What time do you eat lunch/dinner?
B: _____ .
A: When do you finish work/class?
B: _____ .

EXERCISE 5

Listen and fill in the times on the bus schedule. 📼

Bus Schedule

Departures from Dallas	Arrivals in Houston
_____ 6:15 AM	_____ PM
_____ AM	_____ PM
_____ 9:00 AM	_____ 3:00 PM
_____ 12:00 AM	_____ 6:00 PM
_____ PM	_____ PM

EXERCISE 6

Look at the bus schedule in exercise 5 and practice the conversation. 📼

A: Can I help you?
B: Yes. What time does the *first* bus leave for Houston?
A: At _____ .
B: And when does it arrive?
A: At _____ .
B: Thank you.
A: You're welcome.

What's playing tonight?

Gina, Tony, and Pierre are staying in Dallas this weekend. Look at the picture. Then listen as you read the conversation.

Pierre: What's playing tonight?

Tony: Well, there's *The Cowboy Rides Again* with Pat Conroy.

Gina: I don't know. . . . I don't really like westerns.

Pierre: I agree. I don't like westerns very much either. And I don't think Pat Conroy is a good actor.

Tony: OK. What about *Love in the Afternoon*?

Gina: No. I don't like love stories.

Pierre: I don't either.

Gina: Hey! What about *That's a Laugh*? It's a comedy.

Pierre: Yeah. I like comedies. How about you, Tony?

Tony: That's fine with me. I like comedies, too.

Pierre: Keiko?

Keiko: What?

Pierre: Do you like comedies?

Keiko: No. Not really.

Read the conversation on page 89 again and answer *That's right*, *That's wrong*, or *It doesn't say*.

1. Gina likes westerns and love stories.
2. Pierre doesn't like westerns or love stories.
3. Keiko likes westerns and love stories.
4. Gina and Pierre like comedies.
5. Tony doesn't like comedies.
6. Keiko likes comedies.

Look at the chart and make sentences about Gina, Tony, Pierre, and Keiko.

WESTERNS	*Love Stories*	Comedies	Mysteries	Science Fiction	HORROR MOVIES
		Gina		Gina	
Tony	Tony	Tony	Tony		Tony
		Pierre	Pierre		Pierre
Keiko	Keiko			Keiko	

Tony likes westerns. Keiko **does, too.**
Gina doesn't like westerns. Pierre **doesn't either.**

Work in a group. Find out what kind of movies your classmates like. Check (✓) the appropriate movies.

A: **What kind of movies do you like?**
B: **I like** *westerns, science fiction,* **and** *horror movies.*

	Name of Classmate _____	Name of Classmate _____	YOU
Westerns			
Love stories			
Comedies			
Mysteries			
Science fiction			
Horror movies			
OTHER			

EXERCISE 4

Use the information from exercise 3. Make three or four sentences about your group.

Lynn and Yon Mi like westerns and comedies. I like westerns and comedies, too.
Lynn and Yon Mi don't like horror movies. I don't like horror movies, either.
We all like love stories.
No one likes science fiction.

1. _____

2. _____

3. _____

4. _____

Look at each picture. Then choose the best adjective in each sentence.

1. Pat Conroy isn't a (good/bad) actor.

2. Keiko is a (terrible/ beautiful) dresser.

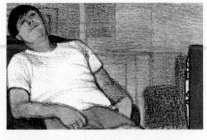

3. Felix isn't a (hard/bad) worker.

4. Tetsuo is a (slow/fast) jogger.

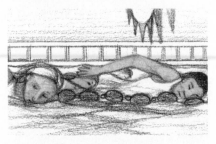

5. Lynn is a (slow/fast) swimmer.

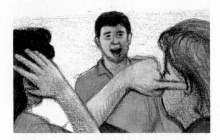

6. Tony is a (good/bad) singer.

7. George isn't a (careful/ terrible) driver.

8. Mrs. Brennan is a (neat/ messy) writer.

Agree with the sentences in exercise 5. Use the verbs and adverbs in the list.

A: Pat Conroy isn't a good actor.
B: I agree. He doesn't **act well**.

A: Keiko is a beautiful dresser.
B: I agree. She **dresses beautifully**.

Verbs	Adverbs
1. act	**well**
2. dress	beautifully
3. work	**hard**
4. jog	slowly
5. swim	**fast**
6. sing	badly
7. drive	carefully
8. write	neatly

A New Job is a comedy. Listen to the actor and actress and write the missing words.

Actor: You're ^{1}____ very good secretary. You work ^{2}____ and you dress ^{3}____ .

Actress: Thank you very much.

Actor: Yes. You type ^{4}____ , you file ^{5}____ , and you answer the phone ^{6}____ .

Actress: Thank you.

Actor: And ^{7}____ speak English very well, ^{8}____ .

Actress: Thank you, but I don't think I understand English very well.

Actor: I don't ^{9}____ . I think ^{10}____ English is very good.

Actress: Well, thank you.

Refer to the conversation in exercise 7 and make sentences about the two secretaries in the comedy. Use your imagination.

> Miss Goodman types neatly, but Miss Michaels doesn't.
> Miss Goodman doesn't dress well, but Miss Michaels does.

LESSON 3

An actor's job isn't easy.

EXERCISE 1

Read the newspaper article about J.C. Kelly.

5 TOWN NEWS • THURSDAY, NOVEMBER 26, 1992

J.C. KELLY—AN ACTOR'S JOB ISN'T EASY

Hollywood—"Every day is a busy day for me," says actress J.C. Kelly. "I get up at six o'clock and exercise for an hour. I go jogging or I swim in my pool. After I exercise, I take a shower and get dressed. Then I have breakfast. After breakfast, I go to the movie studio. I work from eight o'clock in the morning until seven-thirty or eight o'clock at night. It's a long, hard day."

When she gets home, J.C. eats dinner and relaxes with her husband. Sometimes, she watches the news on TV after dinner. Before she goes to bed, she reads her script carefully for the next day. She goes to bed at ten o'clock. "An actor's job isn't easy!" she says.

Now match the first part of each sentence (1–5) with the second part (a–e).

1. Before J.C. goes to work,
2. When she exercises,
3. When she gets home,
4. After she eats dinner,
5. Before she goes to bed,

a. she eats dinner and relaxes.
b. she studies her script for the next day.
c. she exercises and has breakfast.
d. sometimes she watches TV.
e. she jogs or swims.

EXERCISE 2

Look at these sentences. You can write the sentences two ways. Notice the commas (,) in three of the sentences.

> **Before** J.C. goes to work, she exercises and has breakfast.
> J.C. exercises and has breakfast **before** she goes to work.
>
> **When** she gets home, she eats dinner and relaxes.
> She eats dinner and relaxes **when** she gets home.
>
> **After** she eats dinner, sometimes she watches TV.
> Sometimes she watches TV **after** she eats dinner.

Now write about your day. Use the newspaper article in exercise 1 as a model and answer these questions.

1. What time do you get up?
2. What do you after you get up?
3. What time do you work? (from . . . until)
4. What do you do when you get home?
5. What do you do after dinner?
6. What do you do before you go to bed?

Work with a partner. Discuss the movies in the ads. ▭

> A: What's playing tonight at Cinema Six?
> B: *The Last Star* is playing in Theater 1.
> A: What kind of movie is that?
> B: It's *science fiction.*
> A: I love *science fiction.*
>   (I really don't like *science fiction* very much.)
> B: Good. I do, too. (I don't either.)
> A: What else is playing at Cinema Six? . . .

This week Cinema Six presents six great new shows...

THEATER 1

Times _____

_____

Sincerely Yours

THEATER 2

Times _____

_____

The Cowboy Rides Again

THEATER 3

Times _____

_____

THAT'S A LAUGH

THEATER 4

Times _____

_____

THE QUIET HOUSE

THEATER 5   Times   5:00

7:00

9:00

DEAD MEN DON'T TALK

THEATER 6

Times   5:40

7:50

10:00

Listen to the movie announcements. Write the times of the movies. ▭

1. *The Last Star:*   5:30,   7:15,   9:00
2. *Sincerely Yours:*   _____ , _____ , _____
3. *The Cowboy Rides Again:* _____ , _____ , _____
4. *That's a Laugh!:*   _____ , _____ , _____

SIMPLE PRESENT TENSE: INFORMATION (WH-) QUESTIONS

| When | do | you
we
they | leave | for Houston? |
| | does | he
she
the bus | | |

| I
We
They | leave at 9:00. |
| He
She
It | leaves at 9:00. |

How do you go to school?
What time do you go to school?
What kind of movies do you like?

TOO AND EITHER

Gina likes comedies. Pierre likes comedies, **too**.
Gina doesn't like love stories. Pierre doesn't **either**.

ADVERBS OF MANNER

Adjective + -*ly*	Irregular
beautiful**ly**	**well**
slow**ly**	**hard**
bad**ly**	**fast**
careful**ly**	
neat**ly**	

CLAUSES WITH BEFORE, WHEN, AND AFTER

| **Before** Pat goes to work,
When he gets home,
After he eats dinner, | he exercises and has breakfast.
he eats dinner and relaxes.
sometimes he watches TV. |

OR

| Pat exercises and has breakfast
He eats dinner and relaxes
Sometimes he watches TV | **before** he goes to work.
when he gets home.
after he eats dinner. |

actor
again
arrival
bus
cafeteria
cinema
comedy
company
cowboy
departure
dresser
driver
either
horror movie
hour
jogger
laugh
love story
me
movie studio
mystery
phone
pool
really
science fiction
script
show
singer
star
swimmer
tonight
train
until
very much
western
when
worker
writer

A.M. (in the morning)
Hey!
Let's see.
not really
P.M. (in the afternoon/
   at night)
Really?
Thank you very much.

VOCABULARY

VERBS

act
agree
answer
arrive
begin
dress
file
finish
get to (= arrive at)
leave (for)
present
ride
say
sing
speak
swim
type
understand

ADJECTIVES

dead
easy
great
next
terrible

ADJECTIVES → ADVERBS

bad	badly
beautiful	beautifully
careful	carefully
fast	fast
good	well
hard	hard
neat	neatly
slow	slowly

COMMUNICATION SUMMARY

ASKING AND TELLING THE TIME

What time is it?
    It's 9:00.

OFFERING HELP

Can I help you?
    Yes.

ASKING FOR TRANSPORTATION INFORMATION

What time does the next bus leave for Houston?
    At 9:00.
And when does it arrive?
    At 3:00 P.M.

TALKING ABOUT WORK OR SCHOOL

What do you do (for a living)?
    I'm a nurse. (I'm a student.)
Where do you work?
    I work at a hospital in Dallas.
Where do you go to school?
    I go to the University of Texas.
How do you get to work?
    I drive.
What time do you get to work?
    At 8:30.
When do you finish work?
    At 5:00.

DESCRIBING HOW PEOPLE DO THINGS

Keiko dresses beautifully.
Pat Conroy doesn't act well.

CONTRASTING

Miss Goodman writes neatly, but Miss Michaels doesn't.

TALKING ABOUT MOVIES

What kind of movies do you like?
    I like love stories.
What's playing tonight?
    The Last Star is playing in Theater 1.
What else is playing at Cinema Six?

AGREEING

I love science fiction.
    I do too.
I really don't like westerns very much.
    I don't either.

Keiko always works hard.

Look at the picture. Then listen as you read the paragraphs.

Keiko is a secretary. She enjoys her work, and she always works hard. She is always on time for work. In fact, she is often early. She is never late, and she is never sick.

Keiko usually types letters and answers the telephone. She sometimes files and makes copies. She seldom makes mistakes when she types or files. She always answers the phone politely.

Keiko is intelligent, and she has a good sense of humor. She is never angry. Everybody in the office likes Keiko.

Read the paragraphs on page 98 again. Then choose the appropriate adverb of frequency.

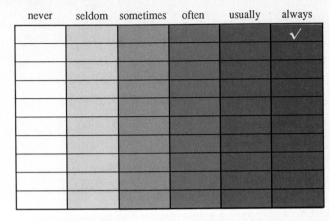

1. Keiko works hard.
2. She is on time for work.
3. She is late or sick.
4. She is early for work.
5. She types letters.
6. She files.
7. She makes copies.
8. She makes mistakes when she types.
9. She answers the phone politely.
10. She is angry.

never	seldom	sometimes	often	usually	always
					✓

Now say the complete sentences. 📼

> 1. Keiko **always works** hard.
> 2. She **is always** on time for work.

3. _____
4. _____
5. _____
6. _____

7. _____
8. _____
9. _____
10. _____

Work with a partner. Talk about these students. Use your imagination. 📼

Keiko is a secretary.
She is **never** late for work.
She **usually** types letters and files.
She **never** makes mistakes when she types.
She **always** answers the phone politely.

1. Tetsuo is a music teacher.
   He is _____ angry.
   He _____ enjoys his work.
   He _____ writes on the blackboard.
   He _____ listens to his students.

(continued)

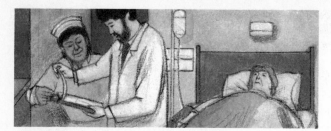

2. Oscar is a doctor and Lucy is a nurse.
   They are _____ tired.
   They _____ make mistakes.
   They _____ go to work at night.
   They _____ work in a hospital.

3. Lynn is a photographer.
   She is _____ unhappy with her job.
   She _____ meets a lot of interesting people.
   She _____ sits at her desk.
   She _____ travels.

4. Pravit is a mechanic.
   He is _____ lazy.
   He _____ wears dirty clothes.
   He _____ works in a garage.
   He _____ fixes cars.

5. Marco is a security guard.
   He is _____ busy.
   He _____ sits down.
   He _____ does dangerous work.
   He _____ works alone.

EXERCISE 3

When Olga is in school, Hector cleans, cooks, and watches the kids. Does he do a good job? Listen and write the sentences. 🔲

1. _____
2. _____
3. _____
4. _____
5. _____
6. _____

Look at the sentences above. Then ask questions about Hector.

A: **How often does Hector** *go to the supermarket?*

B: _____

Pierre is a waiter in a small French restaurant in Dallas. Look at the pictures and complete the sentences about Pierre. Then listen and check your answers.

Pierre **is always** tired, and he **seldom arrives** on time for work.

1. Pierre's customers (often be) hungry, but he (usually sit) and (talk) to his friends in the kitchen.

2. When he (work), he (seldom do) a good job.

3. He (often work) slowly and he (usually forget) his customers' food.

4. He (sometimes drop) food on his customers, and he (never be) polite.

5. But there is one thing Pierre (always remember)— his tip!

Today Pierre's boss is in the restaurant. He is watching Pierre. How is Pierre acting today? Complete the sentences.

Today Pierre is nervous because his boss **is watching.** He **isn't sitting** and **talking** to his friends in the kitchen.

1. Pierre (do) a really good job.
2. He (not work) slowly. He (work) quickly.
3. He (speak) politely and he (help) his customers.
4. But one thing is the same. He (never forget) his tips!

What does Lucy do every day? What is she doing now? Choose the correct form of the verb.

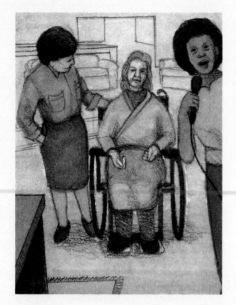

"Lucy Mendoza is a nurse. She is never bored because she is always busy. She usually (1. works/is working) in a hospital, but sometimes she (2. works/is working) in a special home for old people. Lucy (3. enjoys/is enjoying) her work every day, and she never (takes/is taking) a day off. She is always happy. She is never sad. Today she (4. doesn't work/isn't working) in the hospital. She (5. works/is working) in the home for old people. Right now she (6. talks/is talking) to a woman. The woman is very lonely because her children never (7. visit/are visiting)."

> **What about you?**
> What do you usually do every day?
> What are you doing right now?

EXERCISE 7

Find out about different people in your class. 🔲

tired

sick

thirsty

lonely

angry

bored

sad

nervous

A: **Are you ever** *angry*?
B: **Yes. I'm** *often angry*.
   (**No. I'm** *seldom angry*.)

Things we have to do today

Look at the picture. Then listen as you read the conversation.

Jerry: What are you doing, Ann?

Ann: I'm making a list of things we have to do today.

Jerry: And what do *we* have to do today?

Ann: First we have to clean the house. It's really dirty. Then we have to go to the supermarket because we need food for dinner.

Jerry: OK.

Ann: Then we have to go to the post office and buy stamps.

Jerry: Is that all?

Ann: No. Then we have to get gas for the car. It's almost empty.

Jerry: Fine. Then let's go to a movie.

Ann: That's a good idea, but we can't.

Jerry: Why not?

Ann: We have to visit your mother. Today's her birthday!

Jerry: Oh! I always forget!

Read the conversation on page 103 again and complete Ann's list.

THINGS TO DO TODAY

1. _____ the house
2. _____ to the supermarket
3. _____ to the post office
4. _____ gas for the car
5. _____ Jerry's mother

Then ask and answer questions about the list.

A: **Why do they have to** clean the house?
B: **Because** it's dirty.

Look at each statement below. Then ask a question and give an answer.

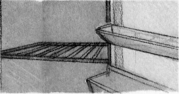

Ann and Jerry need stamps for their letters.
Where **do** they **have to** go?
They **have to** go to the post office.

Tony's refrigerator is empty.
What **does** he **have to** buy?
He **has to** buy food for dinner.

1. Pravit needs some clean clothes. What _____ do? He _____ wash his clothes.

2. Gina's car is almost empty. What _____ do? She _____ get gas for her car.

3. Marco works at night. When _____ get up? He _____ get up at 3:00 P.M.

4. Lucy and her husband don't have any money. Where _____ go? They _____ go to the bank.

5. Tony often makes mistakes. What _____ do? He _____ check his work carefully.

6. Lynn and Keiko have class at 7:00. What time _____ leave their house? They _____ leave at 6:30.

EXERCISE 3

First make a list of four things you have to do tomorrow. Tell your partner what the things are.

> **THINGS I HAVE TO DO TOMORROW**
>
> 1. go to the bank
> 2. study for my English test
> 3.
> 4.

Now find two classmates who have to do the same things you do.

> **A:** Do you have to *go to the bank* tomorrow?
> **B:** Yes, I do. (No, I don't.)

Classmate 1

_____

Classmate 2

_____

EXERCISE 4

Listen and complete the paragraphs.

Jerry Brennan is very ¹_____ during the week. From Monday ²_____ Friday, he gets up ³_____ and goes jogging. Before he leaves ⁴_____ work, he eats a ⁵_____ breakfast and reads the newspaper ⁶_____ .

Jerry drives his taxi ⁷_____ day. Then he goes ⁸_____ the supermarket alone. ⁹_____ he gets home, he ¹⁰_____ dinner for his family. Jerry usually ¹¹_____ to go to bed early ¹²_____ night because he ¹³_____ very tired. ¹⁴_____ today is Saturday and he ¹⁵_____ a day off. He is very ¹⁶_____ .

Now give your opinion. It's Saturday morning. Why is Jerry Brennan happy?

> **I think he's happy because he doesn't have to get up early.**

EXERCISE 5

Work with a group. Make a list of things you *all* have to do during the week but don't have to do on weekends.

> We **have to** get up early during the week, but we **don't have to** get up early on weekends.

Let's have dinner.

EXERCISE 1

Read these ads and then answer the questions.

VILLA ITALIA
A New
Italian Restaurant
401 College Ave. • 555-4700
Open from 11:00 a.m. until 10:00 p.m.

Rock Concert
The
BIG BOYS
sing their new song
YOU'RE DRIVING ME CRAZY
at the
University of Texas
Fri. and Sat.
8:00 p.m. and
10:00 p.m.
808 University Avenue, 555-6000

A GREAT LIFE
5:30, 8:15, 10:30,
Regency Movie Theater
1200 Merrick Ave., 555-4000

The
Philharmonic Orchestra
presents
A classical music concert
8:00 p.m. Thurs., Fri., Sat.
The Dallas Concert Hall
230 Park Avenue
555-7700

UNTIL TOMORROW
6:00, 8:00, 10:00
International Cinema
1230 Merrick Ave., 555-2222

CHEZ MICHEL
Excellent French Food
1123 Lincoln St.
555-2525
Open from
11:30 a.m. to 10:30 p.m.

1. What time does the Italian restaurant open?
2. When does it close?
3. What's the address?
4. Ask about the French restaurant.

5. Where is the Philharmonic Orchestra playing?
6. When is it playing?
7. What number do you call for information?
8. Ask about the rock concert.

9. What kind of movie is *A Great Life*?
10. Where is it playing?
11. What time is it playing?
12. Ask about *Until Tomorrow*.

EXERCISE 2

Listen and complete the telephone conversation.

Man: Let's go to a movie tonight.

Woman: I'm sorry, I can't. [1]_____ .

Man: Oh, I always forget. Well, let's play tennis before you go to class.

Woman: I really can't. [2]_____ .

Man: Well, what about tomorrow? Let's have dinner together. There's a good, new Italian restaurant on College Avenue.

Woman: [3]_____ . [4]_____ ?

Man: How about 7:00?

Woman: [5]_____ ! [6]_____ .

EXERCISE 3

Practice this conversation. Use the ads in exercise 1 or your own ideas.

A: Let's _____ tonight.

B: I'm sorry, I can't. I have to _____ .

A: Well, what about tomorrow? Let's _____ .

B: That's a good idea. What time?

A: How about _____ ?

B: Great! See you _____ .

EXERCISE 4

Read the note below. Then write a note to a friend. Suggest a movie, restaurant, or concert from the ads in exercise 1 or make your own suggestion.

Jim,
Let's have dinner together tonight. There's a good Italian restaurant on College Avenue. It's called Villa Italia. The address is 401 College Ave. Let's meet there at 8:00.
See you later.
Mike

_____,

Let's _____ tonight. There's _____ on (at) _____. It's called _____ (_____ is/are playing). The address is _____ . Let's meet there at _____ . See you later.

_____

EXERCISE 5

Interview people in your class and take notes. Find someone who . . .

Name of Classmate

1. enjoys movies.   _____
2. goes to the movies often. _____
3. often eats in restaurants. _____
4. never eats in restaurants. _____
5. likes rock music.   _____
6. doesn't like rock music. _____
7. is always on time for class. _____
8. is never on time for class. _____
9. has to work on weekends. _____
10. is tired right now.   _____

ADVERBS OF FREQUENCY WITH *BE*

Are you	ever	angry?
I'm	never seldom sometimes often always usually	angry.

ADVERBS OF FREQUENCY WITH THE SIMPLE PRESENT TENSE

How often does he clean the house?		
He	never seldom sometimes often always usually	cleans	the house.

THE SIMPLE PRESENT TENSE VS. THE PRESENT CONTINUOUS TENSE

Pierre usually **sits** and **talks** to his friends in the kitchen.
Today he **isn't sitting** and **talking** to his friends in the kitchen.

HAVE TO

Affirmative Statements

I You We They	**have to**		
He She	**has to**	**go**	to the bank.

Negative Statements

I You We They	**don't have to**		
He She	**doesn't have to**	**go**	to the bank.

Yes/No Questions

Do you **Does** she	**have to**	**work**	on weekends?	Yes,	I do. she does.	No,	I don't. she doesn't.

Information (Wh-) Questions

When	**does** he **do** you	**have to**	**leave?**	At 8:30.

CONJUNCTION: *BECAUSE*

Why do they have to clean the house?
  They have to clean the house **because** it's dirty.

LET'S . . .

Let's go to a movie.
Let's have dinner together.

VOCABULARY

alone
angry
because
bored
classical music
clean
concert
concert hall
copy
customer
dangerous
dirty
during
everybody
excellent
food
home
hungry
information
intelligent
list
lonely
mistake
nervous
old
open
other
philharmonic orchestra
polite
politely
quickly
rock music
sad
sick
song
special

VOCABULARY

stamp
taxi driver
test
thing
thirsty
tip
together
why

a day off
a good sense of humor
I'm sorry, I can't.
In fact,
It's called . . .
on time
See you later.
That's a good idea.
What time?
Why not?

VERBS

buy
check
close
drop
enjoy
forget
get (= buy)
help
make
need
open
remember
travel

COMMUNICATION SUMMARY

TALKING ABOUT HOW OFTEN PEOPLE DO THINGS

She always works hard.
How often does he wash the dishes?
    He seldom washes the dishes.
Are you ever angry?
    No. I'm never angry.

COMPARING

I study English every day.
Right now I'm studying Unit 8.

TALKING ABOUT WHAT PEOPLE HAVE TO DO

What do you have to do tomorrow?
    I have to study for my English test.
Do you have to go to the bank?
    No, I don't.
We have to get up early every day during the week, but we
don't have to get up early on weekends.

ASKING WHY AND GIVING REASONS

Why do they have to clean the house?
    Because it's dirty.

GIVING OPINIONS

I think he's happy because he doesn't have to get up early.

MAKING SUGGESTIONS AND ACCEPTING OR DECLINING

Let's go to a concert tonight.
    I'm sorry, I can't. I have to study.
    That's a good idea.

**LESSON
1**

I'm making a list.

Look at the picture. Then listen as you read
the conversation.

Keiko: What are you doing?

Lynn: I want to make chicken and rice for
dinner, and I need some things from
the grocery store. I'm making a list.

Keiko: Chicken and rice? You mean Lucy's
recipe?

Lynn: Yeah.

Keiko: What's in it?

Lynn: Chicken and rice, of course. And peas,
tomatoes, mushrooms, green peppers,
onions, and garlic.

Keiko: I know we don't have any green peppers
or garlic. And we need some mushrooms,
onions, and peas. But there's some rice
in the cupboard, and there are some
tomatoes in the refrigerator.

Lynn: What about salt and oil?

Keiko: Let's see. We have some salt, but we
don't have any oil.

Lynn: OK. And we need some chicken. Do we
need anything else?

Keiko: Yes. We also need some coffee, orange
juice, and bread for breakfast tomorrow.
And we don't have any milk.

Read the conversation on page 110 again. Then check (✓) the correct items.

	Lynn and Keiko need **some** . . .	do **not** need **any** . . .
1. chicken	____	____
2. rice	____	____
3. peas	____	____
4. tomatoes	____	____
5. mushrooms	____	____
6. green peppers	____	____
7. onions	____	____
8. garlic	____	____
9. salt	____	____
10. oil	____	____
11. coffee	____	____
12. orange juice	____	____
13. bread	____	____
14. milk	____	____

Now write two lists with the words above.

Things you can count

peas

Things you can't count

rice

EXERCISE 2

Look in Lynn and Keiko's cupboards. Ask and answer questions.

A: Is there any *pepper*?
B: There isn't any *pepper*, **but there's some** *salt*.

A: Are there any *peas*?
B: There aren't any *peas*, **but there are some** *beans*.

1. A: bread
   B: bread/rice

2. A: cake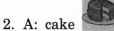
   B: cake/cookies

3. A: coffee
   B: coffee/tea

4. A: potatoes
   B: potatoes/potato chips

5. A: orange juice
   B: orange juice/oranges

6. A: soup
   B: soup/beans

EXERCISE 3

Work with a partner. Look in Keiko and Lynn's refrigerator. Ask and answer questions.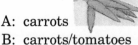

A: Do they have any *orange juice*?
B: They don't have any *orange juice*, **but they have some** *soda*.

1. A: carrots
   B: carrots/tomatoes

2. A: meat
   B: meat/eggs

3. A: bananas
   B: bananas/apples

4. A: oil
   B: oil/butter

5. A: mushrooms
   B: mushrooms/
      lettuce

6. A: milk
   B: milk/
      water

Now ask your partner about the food in his or her kitchen.

Lynn and Keiko are talking about their shopping list. Look at Lynn's answers and ask Keiko's questions.

Keiko: **How many** onions do we need?
Lynn: We do**n't** need **many** onions—only one or two.

Keiko: **How much** garlic do we need?
Lynn: We do**n't** need **much** garlic—only a small package.

There are a lot of mushrooms in this package.

There are not many mushrooms in this package.

There is a lot of orange juice in this bottle.

There is not much orange juice in this bottle.

1. Keiko: _____?
   Lynn: We need a lot of mushrooms—two big packages.

2. Keiko: _____?
   Lynn: We don't need many green peppers—only one or two.

3. Keiko: _____?
   Lynn: We don't need much orange juice—only one small bottle.

4. Keiko: _____?
   Lynn: We need a lot of chicken—two big packages.

5. Keiko: _____?
   Lynn: We don't need many peas—only one can.

6. Keiko: _____?
   Lynn: We don't need any potatoes. We have some.

7. Keiko: _____?
   Lynn: We don't need much oil—only one small bottle.

8. Keiko: _____?
   Lynn: We don't need any rice. We have some.

Nick has a small grocery store in Lynn and Keiko's neighborhood. Ask and answer questions about his store.

A: **Does Nick have** *much oil* **in his store?**
B: **No, he doesn't have** *much oil.*

A: **Does he have** *many beans* **in his store?**
B: **Yes, he has** *a lot of beans.*

Lucy's husband, Simon, owns a supermarket. Listen to the conversation and check (✔) the correct location.

Food	Aisle 1	Aisle 2	Aisle 3
1. oil			
2. salt			
3. pepper			
3. green peppers			
5. onions			
6. mushrooms			
7. coffee			
8. bananas			
9. oranges			
10. chicken			

Now ask where the things are.

A: **Excuse me. Where is/are the _____ ?**
B: **It's/they're in Aisle _____ .**

This week only!

Look at the advertisement. Then listen as you read the prices.

Simon's

SALE THIS WEEK ONLY

Soup
$.79/can

Bread
$1.00/loaf

Jam
$1.87/jar

Butter
$2.09/pound

Lettuce
$.69/head

Oil
$1.65/bottle

Meat
$2.99/pound

Carrots
$.75/bunch

Radishes
$.40/bunch

Eggs
$.98/dozen

Potato Chips
$1.39/bag

Milk
$.99/quart

Cookies
$2.19/box

Read the prices.

49¢
(.49)

MAIN STREET PHARMACY
$1.69

$1.00

KIDS CLOTHES
LAKEVIEW MALL
Size ___ M ___
Price ___ $5.00 ___

SALE 3.02

1. $10.00	2. 75¢	3. $1.50	4. $2.25	5. $13.49
6. $50.00	7. $5.99	8. $16.35	9. $27.10	10. $3.05
11. 10¢	12. $1.00	13. 50¢	14. .25	15. $19.19

EXERCISE 2

Look at the ad for Simon's sale on page 115 and ask about the prices. 📼

A: **How much is** *butter* **this week?**
B: **It's** *$2.09 (two dollars and nine cents) a pound.*

A: **How much are** *eggs* **this week?**
B: **They're** *98¢ (ninety-eight cents) a dozen.*

Match the description with the food.

1. a pound of ___
2. a dozen ___
3. a loaf of ___
4. a head of ___
5. a quart of ___
6. a bag of ___
7. a jar of ___
8. a box of ___
9. a can of ___
10. a bottle of ___
11. a bunch of ___
12. a pound of ___

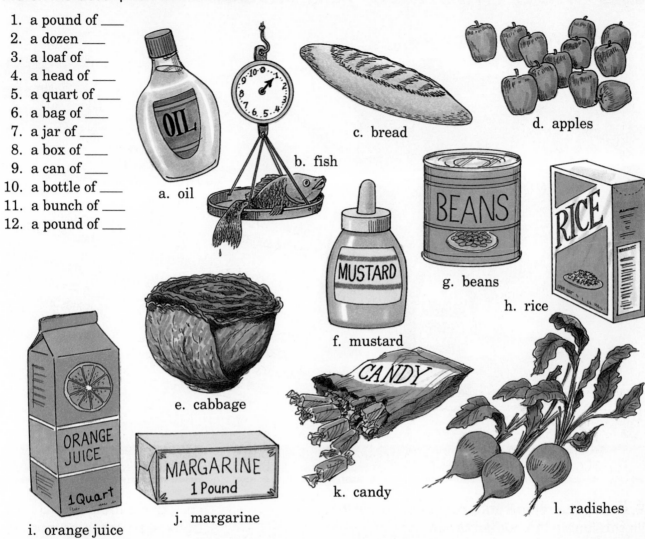

a. oil
b. fish
c. bread
d. apples
e. cabbage
f. mustard
g. beans
h. rice
i. orange juice
j. margarine
k. candy
l. radishes

EXERCISE 4

Work with a group. Ask about prices in the supermarkets in your city. 📼

A: **How much is** *a dozen eggs*?
B: **It's about** *$1.00*.

A: **How much is** *a pound of butter*?
B: **It's about** *$2.20*.

EXERCISE 5

A man is in a small grocery store. Listen to the conversation and write the prices. 📼

eggs ___ a dozen
margarine ___ a pound
cabbage ___ a head
potatoes ___ a bag
bread ___ a loaf
milk ___ a quart

TOTAL ___

Now figure out the price of milk.

LESSON 3 How much do you need?

Listen as you read the recipe.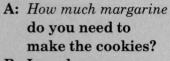

SUGAR NUT COOKIES

1 cup of margarine or butter	2 1/2 cups of flour
1 cup of sugar	2 teaspoons of baking soda
2 eggs	1/2 teaspoon of salt
1 teaspoon of vanilla extract	1 cup of chopped nuts

Heat the oven to 350 degrees. Mix the margarine, sugar, eggs, and vanilla extract in a bowl. Stir in the flour, baking soda, and salt. Then add the nuts. Drop teaspoons of the mixture on a cookie sheet. Bake the cookies for about 10 minutes or until brown. Put the cookies on a plate and cool.

EXERCISE 1

First read the recipe card above. Then put these illustrations in the correct order.

1. **e**   2. ____   3. ____   4. ____   5. ____   6. ____

a

b

c

d

e OVEN

f

EXERCISE 2

Look at the recipe card again and ask questions with *How much* and *How many.*

> **A:** *How much margarine* **do you need to make the cookies?**
> **B: I need** *one cup.*

1. sugar
2. eggs
3. vanilla extract
4. flour
5. baking soda
6. Anything else?

EXERCISE 3

A man and woman are talking. Listen for the missing words.

Man: What are you [1]_____ ?

Woman: My mother's [2]_____ and I have [3]_____ go to the store. [4]_____ making a list. [5]_____ I have to go [6]_____ the bank first. I [7]_____ have any money.

Man: How [8]_____ do you need? I have [9]_____ money.

Woman: Do you have [10]_____ dollars?

Man: Sure.

Woman: Oh, good.

Man: What do [11]_____ need from the store?

Woman: I need some [12]_____ and some orange juice. [13]_____ I also need some [14]_____.

Man: Anything else?

Woman: Yeah. She [15]_____ some ice cream. She likes ice cream [16]_____ she's sick.

Man: OK. Let's go.

EXERCISE 4

Work with a partner. A good friend is very sick and doesn't have any food in the house for dinner. You and your partner have to go to the store for your friend.

1. Decide what you need to buy.
2. Find out the price of each item.
3. Write the total.

SHOPPING LIST	PRICE
_____	_____
_____	_____
_____	_____
_____	_____
_____	_____
_____	_____
Total	_____

EXERCISE 5

Interview your classmates.

A: What's your favorite *fruit?*

B: *Apples.*

What's your favorite . . .	Name of Classmate _____	Name of Classmate _____	Name of Classmate _____
fruit?	_____	_____	_____
vegetable?	_____	_____	_____
meat?	_____	_____	_____
fish?	_____	_____	_____
poultry?	_____	_____	_____
drink?	_____	_____	_____
dessert?	_____	_____	_____

COUNT AND NON-COUNT NOUNS

tomato → tomatoes
rice

SOME AND ANY

Affirmative Statements

There's	**some**	rice in the cupboard.
There are		tomatoes in the refrigerator.

Questions and Negative Statements

Is there	**any**	rice?
Are there		tomatoes?

No,	there isn't	**any**	rice.
	there aren't		tomatoes.

A LOT OF, MUCH, AND MANY

Affirmative Statements

There are	**a lot of**	tomatoes.
There's		rice.

Questions and Negative Statements

Does he have	**many**	beans	in his
	much	oil	store?

No, he doesn't have	**many**	beans.
	much	oil.

QUESTIONS WITH *HOW MUCH* AND *HOW MANY*

How many	onions	do we need?
How much	garlic	

We don't need	many onions.
	much garlic.

QUANTITIES

I have **a box of** rice.
I need **a bunch of** carrots.

a dozen	a can of	a loaf of
a bag of	a cup of	a quart of
a bottle of	a head of	a pound of
a box of	a jar of	a teaspoon of

IMPERATIVE

Bake the cookies for about 10 minutes.
Put the cookies on a plate.

aisle
also
bottle
bowl
box
bunch
can
cent
cookie sheet
cup
degree
dessert
dollar
dozen
favorite
grocery store
½ (a half)
head
jar
loaf
many
minute
mixture
mom
much
only
oven
package
plate
pound
price
quart
recipe
sale
shopping list
spoon
teaspoon
total

Anything else?
of course
Sure.

FOOD

apple
baking soda
banana
bean
bread
butter
cabbage
cake

VOCABULARY

candy
carrot
chicken
coffee
cookies
egg
fish
flour
fruit
garlic
green pepper
ice cream
jam
lettuce
margarine
meat
milk
mushroom
mustard
nut
oil
onion
orange
orange juice
peas
pepper
potato
potato chip
poultry
radish
rice
salt
soda
soup
sugar
tea
tomato
vanilla extract
vegetable
water

VERBS
add
bake
cool
count
heat
mix
put
stir (in)
want (to)

COMMUNICATION SUMMARY

TALKING ABOUT AVAILABILITY

Is there any pepper?
　　There isn't any pepper, but there's some salt.
Does Nick's Grocery Store have much oil?
　　No, it doesn't have much oil.
Do you have any oranges at home?
　　No, I don't.

TALKING ABOUT QUANTITIES

How many onions do we need?
　　We don't need many—only one or two.
How much oil do we need?
　　We need one small bottle.

ASKING FOR LOCATIONS IN A GROCERY STORE

Excuse me. Where's the oil?
　　It's in Aisle 2.

ASKING ABOUT PRICES

How much is a bag of candy?
　　It's 50¢.
How much are eggs this week?
　　They're 98¢ a dozen.

TALKING ABOUT FAVORITE FOODS

What's your favorite fruit?
　　Apples.

Do you have change for a dollar?

Look at the pictures. Then listen as you read the conversation.

Make your selection.

Insert the coins.
(Don't use pennies.)

Press the correct button.

Remove the stamps.

Gina:	Let's see. . . . Insert the coins. Don't use pennies. . . . Oh no! I don't have any change.
Gina:	Excuse me. Do you have change for a dollar? I need change for the stamp machine.
Man:	No, I don't. Sorry.
Gina:	Thanks anyway.
Gina:	Excuse me. Do you have change for a dollar?
Woman:	Yes, I think so. . . . Yes. Here you are.
Gina:	Thank you very much.

Match the pictures with the sentences.

1. Make your selection. <u>c</u>
2. Insert the coins. ____
3. Don't use pennies. ____
4. Press the correct button. ____
5. Remove the stamp. ____

a

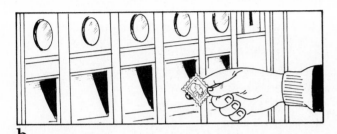

b

c

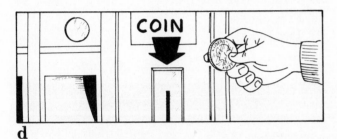

d

e

Look at the pictures and complete the sentences.

Now tell your partner how to use the soda machine.

1. **Make** your selection.
2. ____ the coins.
   ____ ____ pennies.
3. ____ the correct button.
4. ____ the coffee.

5. Make ____ ____ .
6. Insert the ____ .
   Don't use ____ .
7. Press the correct ____ .
8. Remove the ____ .

A: **How do you use this soda machine?**

B: _____

Look at the pictures and practice the words.

a dollar (a one)

a nickel

a quarter

a five

a penny

a dime

a ten

a twenty

Now say the correct coin or bill.

1. Five pennies = *a nickel*
   (Five pennies equal a nickel.)
2. Two nickels or ten pennies =
3. Two dimes and a nickel =
4. Five nickels =
5. Twenty-five pennies =
6. Five ones =
7. Two fives =
8. A ten and two fives =

Work with a group and practice these conversations.

Woman: Excuse me. Do you have change for a *dollar*?
Boy: Yes, I think so. . . . Yes. Here you are.
Woman: Thanks.

Boy: Excuse me. Do you have change for a *quarter*?
Man: No, I don't. Sorry.
Boy: Thanks anyway.

Listen and complete the conversation. 📼

Boy: ¹_____ . _____?
Woman: First decide what you want.
Boy: ²_____ .
Woman: No. Don't press the button.
First insert the coins.
Boy: ³_____ .
Woman: Cookies are fifty cents. Do you
have any change?
Boy: ⁴_____ . _____?
Woman: Yes, here.
Boy: OK. ⁵_____ .
Woman: Right. Then press the button
for cookies.
Boy: ⁶_____ . _____ .
Woman: Hey! What about my quarter?

EXERCISE 6

Practice the conversation in exercise 5. Make your own selection and ask for the change you need.

CANDY	75¢
GUM	25¢
POTATO CHIPS	60¢
COOKIES	50¢

COIN

What are you doing next week?

Look at the picture. Then listen as you read the conversation.

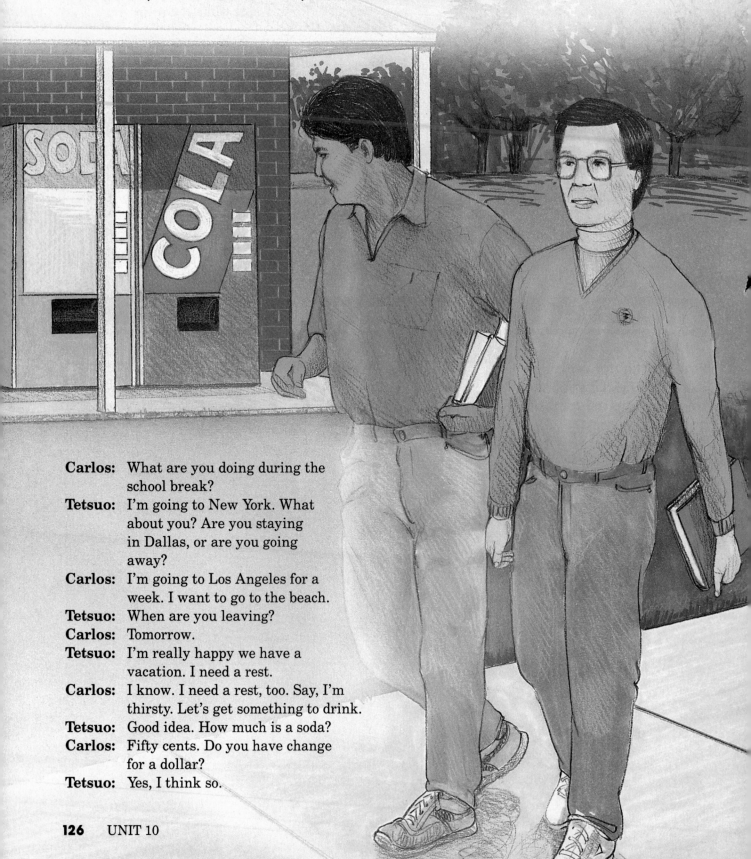

Carlos: What are you doing during the school break?

Tetsuo: I'm going to New York. What about you? Are you staying in Dallas, or are you going away?

Carlos: I'm going to Los Angeles for a week. I want to go to the beach.

Tetsuo: When are you leaving?

Carlos: Tomorrow.

Tetsuo: I'm really happy we have a vacation. I need a rest.

Carlos: I know. I need a rest, too. Say, I'm thirsty. Let's get something to drink.

Tetsuo: Good idea. How much is a soda?

Carlos: Fifty cents. Do you have change for a dollar?

Tetsuo: Yes, I think so.

What do you think? Look at the questions and answer *I think so, I don't think so,* or *I don't know.*

1. Are Tetsuo and Carlos friends?
2. Are there English classes next week?
3. Do Tetsuo and Carlos like to travel?
4. Does Tetsuo like New York?
5. Are there beaches in Dallas?
6. Are Carlos and Tetsuo hungry?

Mrs. Brennan is talking to her class. First, listen and check (✔) *Staying in Dallas* or *Going away.* Then listen again and write the name of the place. 📼

NAME	Staying in Dallas	Going away	Place
1. Tetsuo		✔	New York
2. Keiko			
3. Pierre			
4. Lucy			
5. Carlos			
6. Roberto			
7. Lynn			
8. Mrs. Brennan			

Check your answers with a partner. Use this conversation.

A: Is *Tetsuo* **staying in Dallas or is he going away?**
B: *He***'s going away. (***He***'s staying in Dallas.)**
A: Where's *he* **going?**
B: To *New York***.**

Make conversations like the one below. 📼

A: I'm *thirsty.* **Let's** *get something to drink.*
B: Good idea. How much is *a soda?*
A: *Fifty cents.*

1. A: bored/go to a movie
   B: a ticket
   A: $4.00

2. A: hungry/get a snack
   B: popcorn
   A: $1.00

3. A: hot/get something to drink
   B: soda
   A: $.75

4. A: hungry/buy something to eat
   B: a candy bar
   A: 50¢

5. A: bored/get something to read
   B: a magazine
   A: $1.95

Choose the correct words in the parentheses and complete Tetsuo's letter to his friends in New York.

Dear Maggie and Jim,

I'm coming to New York on Monday. I always (**1.** like/like to) visit New York and see all the people and all the buildings.

I (**2.** need/need to) do some errands in New York, too. I (**3.** want/want to) go to a Japanese bookstore. I (**4.** need/need to) buy some Japanese books and magazines. I (**5.** try/try to) read only English books and magazines, but sometimes I (**6.** need/need to) relax. Then I read Japanese.

Also, I (**7.** want/want to) visit Natsu Tamura. He's working at the Japanese Embassy now. He (**8.** likes/likes to) his job there, but he misses Japan.

Well, I (**9.** have/have to) go now. I'm (**10.** trying/trying to) a recipe for chocolate cake, and it's in the oven. Yes, I (**11.** have/have to) a new hobby — I (**12.** like/like to) cook!

See you soon,

Tetsuo

Work with a group. Interview your classmates and find out what they are doing in the future. Take notes and report your findings to the other groups. Listen to the example.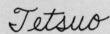

A: **What are you doing** *after class, Carlos*?
B: **I'm** *going home*.
A: **What about you,** *Tetsuo*? **Are you** *going home after class*?
C: *No. I have to work.*

What are you doing . . .	Name of Classmate	Name of Classmate	Name of Classmate
1. after class?			
2. tonight?			
3. tomorrow?			
4. this weekend?			
5. during the next school break?			

Are you ready to order?

Look at the ads and practice the conversation.

A: **What are you doing** *later*?
B: **I'm not doing anything. Why?**
A: **Let's get something to** *eat*.
B: **That's a good idea. Where would you like to go?**
A: **How about** *the Star Restaurant*? **They have** *great hamburgers*.
B: **That's fine.**

Read the menu and answer the questions.

1. What's the special?
2. How many kinds of sandwiches are there?
3. How many kinds of soup?
4. How much is a small salad?
5. How much is a cup of soup?
6. What kind of pie does the restaurant have?

Now ask your own questions about the menu.

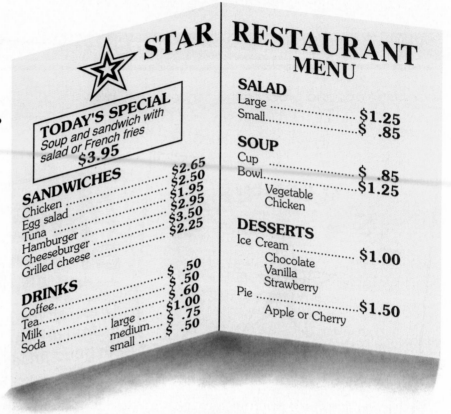

★ STAR RESTAURANT MENU

TODAY'S SPECIAL
Soup and sandwich with salad or French fries
$3.95

SANDWICHES
Chicken $2.65
Egg salad $2.50
Tuna $1.95
Hamburger $2.95
Cheeseburger $3.50
Grilled cheese $2.25

DRINKS
Coffee............ $ .50
Tea............... $ .50
Milk.............. $ .60
Soda   large .. $1.00
          medium . $ .75
          small ... $ .50

SALAD
Large ....
Small............... $1.25
                    $ .85

SOUP
Cup ....
Bowl.............. $ .85
                    $1.25
    Vegetable
    Chicken

DESSERTS
Ice Cream $1.00
    Chocolate
    Vanilla
    Strawberry
Pie $1.50
    Apple or Cherry

Listen and complete the conversation with the kinds of food the customers order.

Waitress: Are you ready to order?
Woman: Yes, I'd like a ^{1}____ and a small ^{2}____ .
Waitress: And how would you like your ^{3}____ ?
Woman: Medium.
Waitress: Anything to drink?
Woman: Just a glass of ^{4}____ .
Waitress: And what would you like?
Man: I'll have a bowl of ^{5}____ soup. And what kind of ^{6}____ do you have?
Waitress: Apple and cherry.
Man: ^{7}____ .
Waitress: Anything else?
Man: Yes. A cup of ^{8}____ .
Waitress: Thank you.

Now practice the conversation.

Complete the check for the man's and woman's lunch. What's the total?

STAR RESTAURANT
Guest Check

Table No.	No. Persons	Check No. 308905	Server No.
	hamburger		2	95
	Total			

Match the questions (1-6) with the answers (a-f).

1. Are you ready to order? __d__
2. Would you like any dessert? ____
3. Anything to drink? ____
4. How would you like your hamburger? ____
5. What would you like? ____
6. What kind of ice cream do you have? ____

a. Medium, please.
b. I'll have a bowl of soup.
c. Vanilla, chocolate, and strawberry.
d. Yes. I'd like an egg salad sandwich.
e. Just a glass of water.
f. Cherry pie, please.

Work with a group. Use the menu on page 130 and write a conversation. Present the conversation to the class.

A: Can I help you?/Are you ready to order?
B: Yes. I'd like/I'll have a *cheeseburger* and *a small salad*.
A: How would you like your *cheeseburger*?
B: Well-done./Medium./Rare.
A: Anything to drink?/Would you like anything to drink?
B: A/Some (drink)./No thanks./Not now, thanks.
A: And what would you like?/And you?
C: I'll have/I'd like (food) and (drink).
A: Anything else?/Would you like anything else?
C: What kind of (dessert) do you have?
A: _____
C: _____

GRAMMAR SUMMARY

AFFIRMATIVE AND NEGATIVE IMPERATIVE

Insert the coins.   **Don't use** pennies.
Push the button.   **Don't push** the button.

VERB + *TO* + VERB

I	**need to** **want to** **try to** **like to**	**buy**	English magazines.

THE FUTURE WITH THE PRESENT PROGRESSIVE TENSE

Are you going away during the school break?
   Yes. **I'm going** to Los Angeles.
When **are you leaving**?
   On Monday.
What **are you doing** after class?
   I'm not doing anything.

EXPRESSIONS OF FUTURE TIME

I'm going to the beach	**later.** **tomorrow.** **tonight.** **next week.** **this weekend.** **after class.** **during the (next) school break.**

VOCABULARY

anything
beach
bookstore
break
button
change
coffee shop
drink
embassy
glass
hobby
just
machine
magazine
medium
ready
rest
selection
something
vacation
visitor

Here you are.
Not now, thanks.
Oh no!
Thanks anyway.

FOOD

candy bar
cheeseburger
cherry
chocolate
french fries
grilled cheese
hamburger
pie
popcorn
salad
sandwich
strawberry
tuna

rare
medium
well-done

COINS

penny
nickel
dime
quarter

VERBS

come
decide
equal
go away
insert
miss
order
press
try (to)
use

ASKING FOR CHANGE

Do you have change for a dollar?
   Yes. Here you are.
Thanks.
Do you have change for a quarter?
   No, I don't. Sorry.
Thanks anyway.

GIVING AND FOLLOWING DIRECTIONS

How do you use this soda machine?
   Decide what you want.
   Insert the coins.
   Don't use pennies.

MAKING SUGGESTIONS

Let's get something to eat.
   Good idea.
How about the Star Restaurant? They have great hamburgers.
   That's fine.

TALKING ABOUT THE FUTURE

What are you doing tomorrow?
   I'm working.
Are you working tomorrow?
   No. I'm going to the beach.

GIVING OPINIONS

I think so.
I don't think so.

ORDERING IN A RESTAURANT

Are you ready to order?
   Yes. I'd like a cup of coffee.
What would you like?
   I'll have a hamburger.
How would you like your hamburger?
   Medium.
Anything to drink?
   No, thanks.
Would you like any dessert?
   What kind of pie do you have?
Apple and cherry.

TAPESCRIPTS
for Listening Comprehension Exercises

UNIT 1

Lesson 1, exercise 5, p. 18

Listen for the missing words.

Mrs. Brennan: Good evening. What's your name, please?
Carlos: Carlos Perez.
Mrs. Brennan: Could you spell your last name, please?
Carlos: P-E-R-E-Z.
Mrs. Brennan: And where are you from?
Carlos: I'm from Colombia.
Mrs. Brennan: Thank you. Please sit down.

Lesson 2, exercise 6, p. 21

Listen and choose the correct response.

1. Where's she from?   (b)
2. Where are they from?   (a)
3. Where are you from?   (a)
4. Where's he from?   (a)
5. Where are you from?   (a)
6. Where's she from?   (a)
7. Where are they from?   (b)
8. Where are you from?   (b)

Lesson 3, exercise 3, p. 23

Listen and write the sentences.

1. How are you?
2. What's your name?
3. It's nice to meet you.
4. Where are you from?
5. Could you spell that, please?
6. What class are you in?

UNIT 2

Lesson 1, exercise 6, p. 30

Listen and choose the correct answer.

1. OK. Let's begin. What's that?   (a)
2. Good. What are those?   (b)
3. Right. What are these?   (b)
4. OK. What's this?   (a)
5. What are those?   (b)
6. Good. And what's that?   (a)

Lesson 2, exercise 3, p. 32

Listen and choose the number you hear.

1. 30   2. 16   3. 50   4. 14
5. 17   6. 80   7. 90   8. 12

Lesson 3, exercise 2, p. 34

Listen and complete the conversation.

Secretary: What's your name?
Mike: Mike Murphy.
Secretary: What's your address?
Mike: 702 Water Avenue, Dallas, Texas. 75201.
Secretary: And your telephone number?
Mike: (214) 555 – 1518.
Secretary: Your place and year of birth?
Mike: Denver, Colorado. 1967.
Secretary: Thank you.
Mike: You're welcome.

UNIT 3

Lesson 1, exercise 7, p. 41

Listen to the sentences. Choose the letter of the sentence you hear.

1. Is this your brother?
2. Yes, it is.
3. Is he married?
4. Yes, he is.
5. Are those his children?
6. Yes, they are.
7. And is your sister married?
8. No, she isn't.

Lesson 2, exercise 3, p. 43

Listen and match the people with the things.

1. Is this your handbag?
   No, it's Lucy's.   (1-c)
2. Is this your money?
   No, it's Tony's.   (2-e)
3. Are these your earrings?
   No. They're Gina's.   (3-h)
4. Is this your briefcase?
   No. It's Mrs. Brennan's. (4-f)
5. Are these your glasses?
   No. They're Lynn's.   (5-a)
6. Are these your gloves?
   No. They're Carlos's.   (6-d)

7. Is this your English book?
   No. It's Olga's.   (7-b)
8. Is this your wallet?
   No. It's Tetsuo's.   (8-g)

Lesson 3, exercise 2, p. 46

Listen and fill in the information.

1. Hello. My name's Roger. I'm from the United States. I'm 35 years old, and I'm a reporter. I'm average height, and I have brown hair and green eyes.
2. Hi. I'm from the United States, too. My name's Ed. I'm 32, and I'm a reporter, too. I'm tall, and I have black hair and brown eyes. Oh, yes, and I have a mustache.
3. Hi. I'm Pamela, and I'm English. I'm 40 years old, and I'm a photographer. I'm short, and I have blue eyes and blond hair.
4. My name's Maria, and I'm from Puerto Rico. I'm 30, and I'm a secretary. I'm tall, and I have red hair.
5. Hi. I'm Julie. I'm Chinese. I'm 29 years old, and I'm a reporter. I'm average height. I have black hair and glasses.

UNIT 4

Lesson 1, exercise 6, p. 53

What is it, and where is it? Listen and complete the sentences.

1. The sofa is between the two doors.
2. There's a chair between the two windows.
3. There's a table behind the sofa.
4. There's a lamp on the table.
5. There's a picture over the sofa.
6. There's a small rug in front of the sofa.
7. There's a TV next to the chair.
8. There's a dog on the rug.

Lesson 2, exercise 3, p. 56

The burglars are in Eddie's bedroom now. Listen and complete their conversation.

Joe: Sssssshhh! Be quiet!
Moe: Is there a television in the room?
Moe: No, there isn't.
Joe: Oh. Well, is there a stereo?
Moe: Yes, there is.
Joe: Good. Are there any pictures on the wall?
Moe: Yes, there are.
Joe: Is there a baseball bat?
Moe: A baseball bat?
Joe: Yeah. A baseball bat. It's for my son!

Lesson 3, exercise 6, p. 59

Listen and complete the postcard.

December 12, 1990
Dear Michio,

How are you? (1) I'm fine. I'm in (2) Boston now. My English class is good. My (3) classmates are nice and (4) my teacher is interesting.

Boston is a (5) big city. There are (6) four seasons here. They (7) are winter, spring, summer, (8) and fall. Right now (9) it's winter and the (10) weather is cold. It's (11) windy and snowy. (12) Please write soon.

                    Your friend,
                    Hiro

UNIT 5

Lesson 1, exercise 5, p. 64

Listen and complete the paragraphs.

Olga isn't having a good day. The kitchen is a mess. The children are fighting. The dog's barking. A salesman is knocking at the door.

Olga is very tired, and she's looking for a babysitter. She's calling her friends, but her friends are busy. She isn't very happy!

Lesson 2, exercise 6, p. 68

Roberto is interviewing Lynn for the school newspaper. Read the questions. Then listen and write the answers.

Roberto: Today I am interviewing Lynn Wang. Hello, Lynn. How are you today?
Lynn: I'm fine, thank you.
Roberto: Are you from Dallas, Lynn?
Lynn: No. I'm from Beijing, China.
Roberto: And what's your profession?
Lynn: I'm a photographer.
Roberto: Are you working here in the United States?
Lynn: Yes, I am. I'm working for a women's fashion magazine.
Roberto: And you're a student, too. Is that right?
Lynn: Yes.
Roberto: What are you studying?
Lynn: I'm studying English at the English Language Institute.
Roberto: Well, your English is very good.
Lynn: Thank you. I have a good teacher.

Lesson 3, exercise 5, p. 71

Listen to the questions about Ana and Silvio Costa and write the answers.

(Example:) Are Silvio and Ana Costa living in Dallas or are they living in Boston?

1. Are Silvio and Ana friends or are they married?
2. Is Ana living with her parents now or is she living with her husband?
3. Are Silvio and Ana living in an apartment or are they living in a house?
4. Is their apartment nice or is it awful?
5. Are they living across from a park or are they living across from a bank?
6. Are they happy in their new apartment or are they unhappy?

UNIT 6

Lesson 1, exercise 4, p. 77

Listen for the missing words.

Ricardo and Ramon are Alicia and George Castro's sons. They go to school. They are twins, and they are in the same class.

Ricardo and Ramon have English, math, and history every day. They have science on Tuesday and Thursday. They have music on Tuesday and Thursday too.

After school, they play with their friends and do their homework. They have dinner with their parents and sister, and then they watch television.

On Saturday morning, they have tennis lessons. On Saturday afternoon, they clean their rooms. On Sunday, they study or go swimming. Sometimes they go to the movies with their parents.

Lesson 2, exercise 5, p. 81

Alicia is talking to a friend. Listen to the conversation and choose the correct answer.

Friend: Do you have any brothers and sisters, Alicia?
Alicia: Yes, I have two brothers, Oscar and Felix.
Friend: Do they live here in Dallas?
Alicia: Oscar lives here, but Felix lives in Denver.
Friend: What's Oscar like?
Alicia: He is very serious. He works hard and studies a lot.
Friend: What's Felix like?
Alicia: Felix is different. He's lazy. He stays home and watches TV all day.

Lesson 3, exercise 1, p. 82

Listen and write the sentences.

(Example:) Susan doesn't work on the weekend.

a. We go jogging in the park.
b. She works at the hotel every day.
c. She doesn't have any sisters.
d. Susan's from New York.
e. And she likes school.
f. She stays home and studies.

UNIT 7

Lesson 1, exercise 5, p. 88

Listen and fill in the times on the bus schedule.

Agent: Can I help you?
Man: Yes. What time is the first bus to Houston?
Agent: Let's see. The first bus leaves Dallas at 6:15 in the morning, and it arrives in Houston at 12:15 in the afternoon.
Man: And the next bus?
Agent: Well, the next bus leaves Dallas at 8:45 in the morning. That bus arrives in Houston at 2:45 in the afternoon. Then there is a 9:00 bus. It arrives at 3:00 in the afternoon. And there is a 12:00 bus. It arrives at 6:00 at night.
Man: When does the last bus leave?
Agent: At 3:25 P.M. It arrives in Houston at 9:25 at night.
Man: Thank you.
Agent: You're welcome.

Lesson 2, exercise 6, p. 93

A New Job is a comedy. Listen to the actor and actress and write the missing words.

Actor: You're a very good secretary. You work hard and you dress neatly.
Actress: Thank you very much.
Actor: Yes. You type fast, you file carefully, and you answer the phone well.
Actress: Thank you.
Actor: And you speak English very well, too.
Actress: Thank you, but I don't think I understand English very well.
Actor: I don't agree. I think your English is very good.
Actress: Well, thank you.

Lesson 3, exercise 4, p. 95

Listen to the movie announcements. Write the times of the movies.

Tonight Cinema Six is happy to present six great new movies. In Theater 1, we have *The Last Star*, a new science fiction movie. *The Last Star* is playing at 5:30, 7:15, and 9:00.